Sue Clutterham

Scripture Union

For Terry, Lucy and Anna

With thanks to Terry Clutterham, Geoff Harley-Mason, Carol Leetch and Dave Richards who developed the original concept so creatively.

Very special thanks to the members of Knowle Parish Church who took a deep breath and a lot of risks, and worked so hard to make it all happen.

Copyright © Sue Clutterham 1997
First published 1997, reprinted 1998
ISBN 1 85999 097 5

Scripture Union, 207-209 Queensway, Bletchley,
Milton Keynes, MK2 2EB

British Library Cataloguing-in-Publication Data
A catalogue record for this book is available from the British Library.

Design by Patricia Donnelly Graphic Design, London
Illustrations by Colin Smithson
Cover design by Keith Jackson

Printed and bound in Great Britain by Ebenezer Baylis

GET THE TROPICAL FLAVOUR!

Relax, lie back in your deck-chair and sip a long, refreshing drink. Hear the gentle waves lapping gently on the shore and feel the balmy breeze caressing your face. Yes, you're **GOING BANANAS!**

Welcome to the exotic holiday club package with a tropical feel and the emphasis definitely on holiday! Courtesy of Anywhere Airways, five to eleven year olds fly off to Banana Island where they will learn about God in a relevant, exciting and fun-filled way.

Your holiday club venue will first become the airport departure lounge to which the Passengers (children) gain access via Passport Control (registration). They will then sit with their Cabin Crew (group leaders) in the specially chartered 747 waiting for take-off.

To begin each day's programme, the Captain (club co-ordinator) talks the Passengers through their 'flight' to Banana Island. As they touch down, the Banana Boys (two pantomime-style characters) appear to present the rest of the programme from

the beach (stage area). The venue has now become Banana Island. These are leaps of imagination that children find much easier to make than adults do!

NOT-SO-LAZY TROPICAL DAYS

The visit to the island includes singing with the Banana Band, a Bible story from the **GOING BANANAS!** video, Banana Bunches (small-group times), Banana Splits (refreshments), Bananabrains (a quiz), Mashed Bananas (games), Banana Skins (zany activities) and Bananaerobics. No one will want to miss the Time Shed with all its strange surprises. While all this is going on, the Cabin Crew and Passengers need to watch out for the Banana Piranha! To follow up the day's teaching, every passenger completes a Postcard Home. At the end of the session, the Passengers take the 'return flight' before Disembarkation (dismissal). The Passengers exit through Passport Control to await collection by their families.

Primarily an outreach programme for unchurched children, **GOING BANANAS!** aims to teach them basic truths about God and introduce them to him through Jesus. The Bible characters they will meet during the week may seem to have 'gone bananas', but in fact the sanest thing that anyone can do is to love and trust God, and to live his way.

Contents

Going Bananas

MORE THAN JUST A WEEK OF TROPICAL FUN!

GOING BANANAS! is designed to be part of an ongoing strategy for work with children in a church setting. It is relatively easy to organize something successful, zany and exciting that attracts large numbers who normally never come to church, but the important consideration is what will have happened to these children a year later. Your planning should be long-term.

GETTING STARTED

Make sure you begin your planning by answering these questions:

How committed can your church be to maintaining contact with the children who attend?

What provision will you make for unchurched children who are unable to attend on a Sunday?

Can the church arrange follow-up activities for the children which will include their families?

this holiday club. Ideally it will also be the destination, as children who attend decide that they want to continue to take part in church activities.

Before you go any further, the most important thing to do is pray. Gather a small planning group together and work through pages 6 to 22 of this resource with them. Either use it as it stands or adapt it where necessary to suit your church situation and the specific group of children you hope to reach. If you pray, plan and prepare thoroughly, you will be less likely to panic!

Discuss these questions with your church leader. If you discover that you do not have a strategy for integrating unchurched children, do something about it before you go any further.

Clear aims and objectives are crucial for effective and strategic planning. Perhaps **GOING BANANAS!** could give a boost to your existing children's work or be the start of a new venture, such as a midweek club. Your church is not only the starting-point for

THE TOTALLY TROPICAL TEAM

Your most valuable resource will be the team of volunteers who are prepared to get stuck in with **GOING BANANAS!** You will need people to fill the following roles:

Control Tower
The prayer group that gives invaluable support for the whole event as it is happening, praying both for specific activities and also for the children and team members by name.

Captain
The overall co-ordinator of the holiday club, who also talks everyone through the take-off and landing procedure for the outward and return flights each day, using the script on page 17.

Navigator
The person who does Talk Time as part of the Bible teaching, with ability to communicate well with children.

Passport Control
The organisers of the daily registration system for the arrival and departure of the Passengers (children).

Cabin Crew
The team members who are responsible for the Passengers in their Banana Bunches (small groups divided by age, if appropriate, with at least two adults per group).

Airport Staff
Assistant team members (possibly older teenagers) who help with Passport Control by welcoming the Passengers, escorting them and introducing them to their Cabin Crew, joining in with Banana Bunches during the session and doing essential supportive work like taking Passengers to the toilet.

Banana Boys
Can be girls! The double act that strings the programme together, introducing each item and making appropriate links. They are banana growers who live on Banana Island. They keep their tools in a shed which is, in fact, a Time Shed. Working on the same principle as the tardis from the *Dr Who* series, it can travel backwards and forwards in time – with sound effects and lighting of course! The Time Shed is the biggest stage prop used by Bananadrama.

Bananadrama
The actor, or small group of actors, that performs the sketch relating to each day's Bible story, as appropriate Bible characters appear out of the Time Shed to be interviewed by the Banana Boys.

Bananas Wired for Sound and Light
The team responsible for obtaining, setting up and operating the video, overhead projector and screen, sound effects, lighting and public address (PA) system.

Banana Band
A group of confident musicians, preferably with a steel-band style to add to the atmosphere.

Banana Splits
The refreshments team.

Yes, We Have Some Bananas!
The props department, responsible for everything from name badges, costumes, decorations for the venue and construction of the stage set, to supplying Passport Control with Passports and the Cabin Crew with all the photocopied sheets and Postcards Home they will need each day. Yes, We Have Some Bananas! will also be responsible for topping up each Banana Bunch's resource box with crayons, paste, scissors and other craft resources.

LET'S GET LEGAL!

The welfare of the children we are hoping to reach through **GOING BANANAS!** is of paramount importance. We are concerned for their spiritual welfare, but equally important is their physical and emotional welfare. Sadly nowadays, children are at risk more than ever before, and it is our duty to do all we can to ensure their safety and well-being as we aim to show them God's love.

As good practice, all team members need to be made aware of the current legislation arising from the *Children Act 1989*. The issues that affect **GOING BANANAS!** are to do with day-care of children, especially relating to children under eight years old, but they are appropriate for all children attending a church-run event. The following guidelines must be taken into consideration during your initial planning:

- You may need to register **GOING BANANAS!** with Social Services if you use your premises for more than two hours in a day. Officially, the **GOING BANANAS!** programme runs for exactly two hours, but the children can join in with an organised activity as soon as they arrive – usually earlier than the start time. Any holiday club which runs for more than six days in a year must be registered, so if you are planning follow-up events, it might affect you. Phone Social Services and check with the Local Day Care Advisor – he or she is there to help!

- Requirements for accommodation state that the premises should be warm and adequately lit and ventilated. Minimum unencumbered floor space to be provided for children aged 5-8 years is 25 square feet (2.3 square metres) per child. In other words, be careful about very large numbers of children in a small hall and work out the maximum number of children who can attend.

- The premises you use will need to meet the Health and Safety requirements, so check that the owners of the premises have complied with all the requirements. Ideally there should be one toilet and one handbasin for every ten children. Disposable towels or hot-air hand driers are preferable to roller towels.

- If you are preparing food on site, you will need to be inspected by the Environmental Health Office. Ideally, any sandwiches should be refrigerated (for example, if the children bring packed lunches). Smoking should not be permitted on the premises.

- Any accidents or incidents occurring during a session must be recorded in an Accident Book. This is essential in the event of any insurance claim. A record of the matter should be noted, along with details of the action taken. It should be countersigned where appropriate.

- Everyone should be made aware of emergency procedures and fire exits, and there must be access to a telephone. This could be a mobile phone, if necessary. A first aid kit must be kept to hand and at least one member of your team should have a working knowledge of first aid.

- All groups need liability insurance. Make sure your activity is adequately covered by your church's policy.

- Recommendations for adult to child ratios are as follows:
    For 0-2 years
    – one adult to every three children (1:3)
    For 2-3 years
    – one adult to every four children (1:4)
    For 3-8 years
    – one adult to every eight children (1:8)
    For over eights
    – one adult for the first eight children, followed by one for every twelve (1:12).

- There should always be more than one adult for any group and one should be female. Let your team members know that it is not appropriate for them to talk to children alone in a secluded place – it might be misinterpreted. Do not allow people not known to you to have unsupervised access to the children. Sadly, touching children is not advisable now, although a female leader comforting a distressed young child with a cuddle would not be considered inappropriate. It is a question of common sense in this area, but if in doubt, don't!

CONFIDENTIAL DECLARATION FORM FOR POTENTIAL TEAM MEMBERS

All employed people with access to children (that is, anyone under the age of eighteen) have, by law, to make a signed declaration of any criminal record. A key recommendation in *Safe from Harm* (HMSO) also requires such a statement from volunteers. Failure to take the necessary steps could lead to a claim of negligence against the church if a child comes to any harm at the hand of anyone working with them in a voluntary capacity. 'Harm' includes ill-treatment of any kind (including sexual abuse), or impairment of physical or mental health or development.

- You should ask all potential team members to sign the form below.
- When using such a form, emphasise that it represents positive action for good practice, and slur or suspicion is not implied. Obviously the nature of the form is sensitive and should be handled with care.
- Ensure that confidentiality is maintained. In accordance with the Data Protection Act, do not divulge any information to third parties.
- If anyone gives a 'yes' answer, allow the individual to explain this disclosure personally or by letter. If you are in any doubt about the person's suitability, consult your church leader.
- As well as the declaration form, it is recommended that potential team members offer one name as a referee. Questions to ask a referee might include:

  - In what capacity have you known the applicant, and for how long?
  - How willing and able is he/she to work with others?
  - How suitable would you consider him/her for work with children and young people?
  - Are there any relevant details about this applicant which cause you concern?

CONFIDENTIAL DECLARATION

Guidelines from the Home Office following the *Children Act 1989* advise that all voluntary organisations, including churches, take steps to safeguard the children who are entrusted to their care. You are therefore asked to make the following declaration:

Have you ever been convicted of a criminal offence (including any 'spent convictions' under the Rehabilitation of Offenders Act 1974*) or been cautioned by the police or bound over to keep the peace?

☐ Yes

☐ No

Have you ever been held liable by a court for a civil wrong, or had an order made against you by a matrimonial or a family court?

☐ Yes

☐ No

Has your conduct ever caused, or been likely to cause harm to a child or put a child at risk, or, to your knowledge, has it ever been alleged that your conduct has resulted in any of these things?

☐ Yes

☐ No

Signed ———————————————————

Date ———————————————————

* Because of the nature of the work for which you are applying, this post is exempt from the provision of Section 4(ii) of the Rehabilitation of Offenders Act 1974, by virtue of the Rehabilitation of Offenders Act 1974 (Exemptions) Order 1975, and you are therefore not entitled to withhold information about convictions which, for other purposes, are 'spent' under the provisions of the Act. In the event of an appointment, any failure to disclose such convictions could result in the withdrawal of approval to work with children in the church.

TEAM TRAINING SESSIONS

Once you have a group of people willing to get stuck in with **GOING BANANAS!** your main priority will be to build them into a team. Whether they have responded to an appeal for help, or you have approached them individually, they will need to be trained for the task.

Ideally, you need at least two compulsory team training sessions – perhaps one evening meeting, followed by a day for prayer and preparation. You should cover the following:

- Team building (for instance, an activity or shared meal)
- Bible focus and prayer, looking at the aims and objectives (see 'Why and how?' below)
- Guidelines for building relationships with the children (see 'Dos and don'ts' below)
- A look at the programme, including a run-through of the first day (page 23)
- Allocation of roles and responsibilities (page 6)
- Organising the practicalities (page 14)
- Learning the songs (pages 11 and 62)
- Explaining Christian truth to children (page 62)
- Discipline (see 'Dos and don'ts' below)
- Safety and emergency policy
- Specific prayer for the event and the children
- Follow-up strategy

WHY AND HOW?

Why? The aims of **GOING BANANAS!** are set out on page 10.
How? The diagram (which can be enlarged and copied onto an overhead projector acetate) illustrates how we can achieve these aims. The accompanying verses form the basis for the team Bible focus – they could be studied in three groups.

Building quality relationships
1 John 3:11,18, 4:7
We need to accept the children, pray for them and show them God's love.

Communicating Christian truth
Deuteronomy 6:6-9, 31:12-13; Luke 2:46;
2 Timothy 3:15
We communicate it not only through the video story, but also through songs, prayers, the Time Shed interviews and Banana Bunch activities.

Embodying Christian lifestyle
Philippians 2:1-16; John 10:10b
Jesus, the servant King, gives us the perfect example.

DOS AND DON'TS FOR BANANA BUNCHES

Get all the team into small groups to brainstorm on this, then feed back to the whole team. The ideas below are the sort of points to cover:

- **Do** direct the children's attention to what is going on at the front.
- **Don't** forget the children's names. Learn them and use them.
- **Do** encourage them to join in, and make sure you join in with everything too.
- **Don't** forget the quiet or shy children. Be on the look-out for them and sit with them.
- **Do** split up disruptive or restless children and sit with, or between them, if necessary.
- **Don't** leave the group alone unless really necessary. Airport Staff take children to the toilet.
- **Do** make sure that only one person talks at a time – perhaps when they are holding a banana?
- **Don't** hang around the edge of the room, chatting – there is time for that afterwards.
- **Do** pray for the children.

THE BIBLE MATERIAL

GOING BANANAS! aims to introduce Jesus to children who do not yet know him and to strengthen the faith of those who do. We catch a glimpse of what God is like in the lives of some Old Testament characters; we get the full picture of what he is like in Jesus.

These two aims can be achieved in the Banana Bunches (small groups) by:

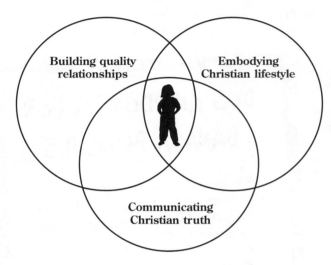

It is not only the Bible teaching that is important. The care shown to the children and the quality of all the other activities should also give a clear, positive message. The main emphasis should be on the relationships in the small groups, between all the group members. There needs to be an 'in it together' feel, with everyone – children *and* adults – joining in the fun and learning new things about God.

GOING BANANAS! is a five-day programme. Each day focuses on a character from the Bible who, for some reason, 'went bananas' for God – Noah, Gideon, Elijah, Zacchaeus and 'Jemima', the woman with the jar of perfume. A 'grand finale' on the following Sunday would be a good opportunity to invite the children and their families to church. (There are suggestions for an all-age worship session on page 61.) The accompanying **GOING BANANAS!** video covers all the biblical material and although it is not essential, it is a highly recommended resource. If you are not able to use the video for your event, use that slot in the programme to tell the appropriate Bible story.

THE SHAPE OF A DAY'S PROGRAMME

Banana Bunches set the scene with an introductory game. The video presentation tells the Bible story and is followed by the Time Shed sequence, when the Banana Boys interview the featured Bible character. Talk Time, given by the Navigator, sums up everything before the Banana Bunches have a chance to chat about what they have heard and seen. They discuss all or some of the following questions:

All these (with the possible exception of 4) are good questions to ask of any Bible passage because the Bible reveals who God is and how he wants us to live. The **GOING BANANAS!** team teaches the children to handle the Bible for themselves as they model basic Bible interpretation.

In Banana Bunches, those who want to can write or draw the group's answers to the six questions on blank speech bubbles, to be displayed on the walls of the venue the next day. The Postcards Home reinforce an aspect of the day's teaching. Younger children, or those with learning difficulties, may need help with these. This will give the Cabin Crew an opportunity to work with them on a one-to-one basis.

If some older children feel they are too grown-up to join in with the Banana Bunch activities, they could have special tasks such as making a simple video of the event, interviewing some of the children and adults to find out what they have learnt about God, or helping Banana Splits with the refreshments. They could also be responsible for displaying each day's speech bubbles on the walls.

Going Bananas Song

Verse

Here we are down by the sea,
Gathered here for all to see,
Here to learn about our King,
So clap your hands and let's all sing.

Chorus

Down by the sea – we're going bananas!
Come, follow me – we're going bananas!
That's where I'll be – going bananas!
We're meeting Jesus.

Ba ba ba ba
Ba ba ba ba
GOING BANANAS!

©1995 Rachael Jones

12

SUGGESTED LAYOUT of VENUE

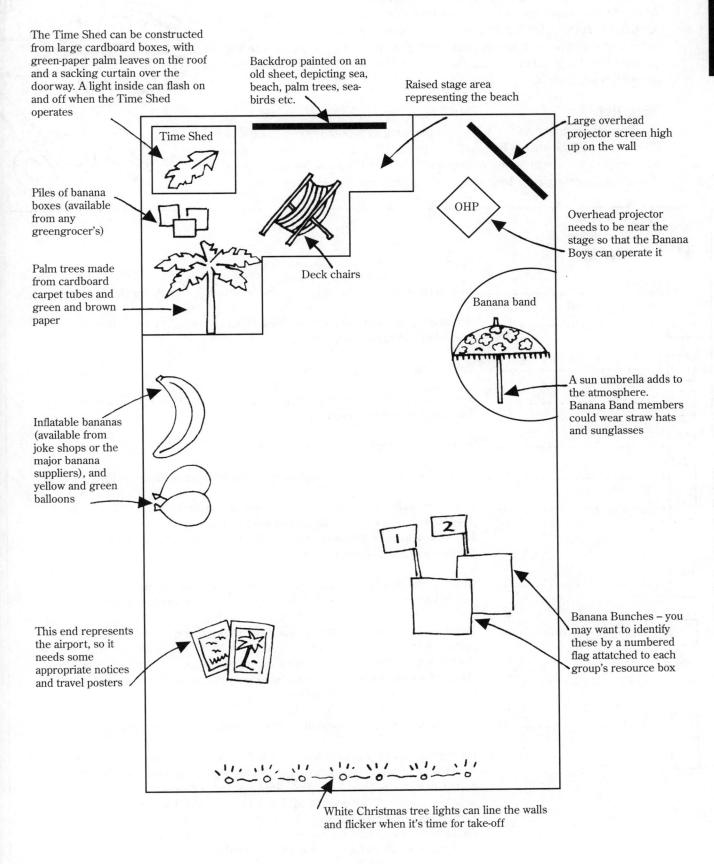

The Time Shed can be constructed from large cardboard boxes, with green-paper palm leaves on the roof and a sacking curtain over the doorway. A light inside can flash on and off when the Time Shed operates

Backdrop painted on an old sheet, depicting sea, beach, palm trees, sea-birds etc.

Raised stage area representing the beach

Large overhead projector screen high up on the wall

Time Shed

Piles of banana boxes (available from any greengrocer's)

OHP

Overhead projector needs to be near the stage so that the Banana Boys can operate it

Palm trees made from cardboard carpet tubes and green and brown paper

Deck chairs

Banana band

A sun umbrella adds to the atmosphere. Banana Band members could wear straw hats and sunglasses

Inflatable bananas (available from joke shops or the major banana suppliers), and yellow and green balloons

1 2

This end represents the airport, so it needs some appropriate notices and travel posters

Banana Bunches – you may want to identify these by a numbered flag attatched to each group's resource box

White Christmas tree lights can line the walls and flicker when it's time for take-off

Practicalities

Behind the scenes

The secret of organising a holiday club successfully is to be adaptable. Work with what you have, not what you wish you had! For instance, if the suggested layout for **GOING BANANAS!** is impractical for your venue, change it. Juggle the programme and adapt it to suit your particular situation. But make sure you are prepared well in advance, so that there is still time for last-minute alterations and unforeseen hitches.

Task list

Go through the practicalities with your planning group and draw up a list of people who will be able to help with the tasks. Allocate at least one person to each job. Some of these will be the responsibility of Yes, We Have Some Bananas! but it's worth allocating each task specifically so that nothing is overlooked.

✔	NAME	TASK
☐	-------------------------	Beg, borrow or buy all the resources and props needed for the week.
☐	-------------------------	Set up the stage area and the Time Shed. Obtain carpet tube(s) and make palm tree(s), as shown on venue layout.
☐	-------------------------	Paint a backdrop using an old sheet.
☐	-------------------------	Produce notices for the Airport such as 'Passport Control' and 'All Passengers This Way' (best done on a computer).
☐	-------------------------	Arrange the venue and move furniture where necessary.
☐	-------------------------	Decorate the venue with balloons, posters, inflatable bananas and notices.
☐	-------------------------	Make a checklist and photocopy all the Banana Bunches' session resource material needed in appropriate quantities (remembering that Cool Shades and the Postcards Home need to be photocopied onto thin card), and sort them into Banana Bunch bundles for each day's programme.
☐	-------------------------	Organise the printing of t-shirts for team members, using the master on page 16. Yellow bananas printed on a black t-shirt produce a very striking effect.
☐	-------------------------	Put together costumes for the Banana Boys (baggy shorts, brightly coloured t-shirts and straw hats), the Captain (peak cap and navy jacket, both with gold braid stuck or sewn on), the Time Shed characters (gowns and headgear can be made from sheeting, towels or plain bed covers) and Passport Control (black or navy skirts or trousers, white shirts, yellow neck scarves).
☐	-------------------------	Make enough badges for team members and children, plus extra for spares.
☐	-------------------------	Put together a basic resource box for each Banana Bunch, with a numbered flag attached to the side so that it is easy to identify separate groups. Each box should contain at least one *Good News Bible*, thick and thin felt-tip pens, crayons if required, pencils and a pencil sharpener, a stapler and staples, a reel of sticky tape, a supply of scrap paper and a cloth for mopping up any spills. The specific materials needed for each activity will be supplied by Yes, We Have Some Bananas! who will be responsible for checking the Equipment Needed list daily.

☐ ------------------------- Make the Message in a Bottle system by collecting well in advance at least five large, empty, clean plastic bottles (one for each day that it happens plus a spare). The two- or three-litre bottles of fizzy lemonade available from supermarkets are best. The larger the better, and if they are green they will be more authentic. You will also need a large fishing net. Provide small sheets of paper and pens for the Passengers' messages, which they roll up and post in the bottle.

☐ ------------------------- Make a Banana Bin with banana-shaped, yellow pieces of paper.

☐ ------------------------- Buy and organise the refreshments for Banana Splits.

☐ ------------------------- Make the Banana Piranha sock puppet needed for the Bananabrains quiz. Use an old yellow sock and fix eyes and suitably sharp white teeth to it. Collect enough bunches of five bananas, for one bunch per Banana Bunch, as well as a True and False card each. The Banana Boys need a fruit basket.

☐ ------------------------- Obtain from your local library BBC sound effects tapes of aeroplane noises, seaside sounds (eg, waves and seagulls) and suitable noises or music for the time-travel sequence. Prepare the pre-recorded material needed for the take-off and landing sequences each day, and for the Time Shed routine. Do several practice run-throughs to check the timing.

☐ ------------------------- Collect all the materials you will need for Banana Bunches 1 on the last day, when the Passengers dress up as party guests, either in biblical or modern-day costumes. Ask your church members to provide old sheets, plain tea towels, bed covers and anything else that would make robes and head-dresses. For the modern outfits, you will need large black and green bin liners, and as many other colours of bin liner that you can find. You will also need coloured tissue and crêpe paper, silver foil, paper doilies, string and ribbon, as well as elastic, triangles of paper and cotton wool for beards or use face paints, or both! You will also need to fix everything together with lots of sticky tape, a stapler and safety pins.

☐ ------------------------- Prepare the Passports (photocopied on yellow paper from pages 20 and 21) and set up Passport Control (see page 22).

☐ ------------------------- Set up the electrical equipment, including the overhead projector and screen, the video system, Christmas tree lights around the edge of the venue, and a sound system if you are using one. Make sure it is safe, with all leads well covered, and have spare bulbs and fuses handy.

☐ ------------------------- Rehearse the Banana Band and write or photocopy all the song words onto overhead projector acetates, checking your church's CCL copyright licence.

☐ ------------------------- Prepare all the Banana Boys' props needed during the week, and rehearse the script routines and Time Shed interviews.

☐ ------------------------- Obtain a suitable workout tape and prepare a simple routine for Bananaerobics.

☐ ------------------------- Produce a prayer leaflet with all the names of team members and children listed. Distribute to the Control Tower staff, church members and others who will pray for you.

☐ ------------------------- Nominate someone who is suitably qualified to be in charge of first aid and assemble a first aid kit, making sure all the team know where it will be kept.

☐ ------------------------- Appoint someone to be responsible for all the publicity and advertising.

T-SHIRT MASTER

T-shirts are an optional extra, but they are a good way of identifying team members, as well as adding to the general atmosphere. Check your local Yellow Pages for addresses of printers, and shop around for a good quote. All team members should have one (except those in specific costumes) and they could be asked to contribute towards the cost. Black t-shirts are best and do not show the dirt!

CAPTAIN'S SCRIPT

Take-off procedure

If preferred, the Captain can ad lib at this point in the programme, or use the script as a rough guideline, varying it slightly each day. It should be a send-up of the patter the pilot normally delivers in a monotone over the intercom. If someone is available (perhaps one of the Passport Control staff) to pose as an air steward or stewardess and do a spoof routine for the instructions, it will all add to the fun. He or she must assume a fixed smile, wave his or her arms about to indicate the emergency exits, demonstrate the use of a life jacket if available (anyone into water sports or sailing may have one), and produce an oxygen mask constructed from a plastic cup and a piece of elastic.

Captain: Good morning, ladies and gentlemen. This is your Captain speaking. Welcome aboard Anywhere Airways flight 123 to Banana Island. At present the plane is taxiing along the runway, waiting for clearance for take-off. We shall be cruising at an altitude of approximately ten centimetres. Will all passengers please note the location of the emergency exits and the toilets. *(At this point, the steward(ess) indicates the real fire exits and toilets.)* May I remind passengers that the toilets may only be used during the Banana Splits refreshment break. In the event of an emergency, you will find a life jacket under your seat. Should the pressure inside the cabin fall for any reason, oxygen will be supplied automatically. Pull down the mask, place it over your face and breathe normally. Ladies and gentlemen, please fasten your seat belts and make sure your seats are in the upright position. I hope you have a very pleasant flight with us on Anywhere Airways. *(The main lights are dimmed, the runway lights come on and the sound effects tape of a plane taking off is played.)*

Captain: Ladies and gentlemen, we are approaching Banana Island after a very brief and uneventful flight. Please fasten your seat belts for our descent. The temperature on the ground is approximately thirty degrees. When we land on Banana Island, please watch out for the banana growers known as the Banana Boys. One is lazy, the other is bossy, and they never get their bananas picked on time. Thank you. *(Exits.)*

(The main lights come on, the runway lights are off and the sound effects tape of waves and seagulls begins.)

SKETCH FOR PROMOTING GOING BANANAS!

This sketch needs the Captain and someone dressed as a holidaymaker, in sunglasses, shorts, t-shirt and sandals, with a beach towel slung over their shoulder. As many bananas as possible should be placed around the venue before the children arrive. You will need enough invitations for every child to have one each, plus some extra copies.

Captain: Hello, everyone. It's lovely to be with you today...

Holidaymaker: *(Hurrying in, oblivious of the Captain.)* I'm sure it's here somewhere. It must be! Perhaps it's behind here... No? Well, maybe it's here then...

Captain: Err... Excuse me. What are you doing?

Holidaymaker: What am I doing? I'm looking for the tropical island of course!

Captain: Tropical island?

Holidaymaker: Yes!

Captain: *(Laughing nervously.)* Tropical island... *here*?

Holidaymaker: *(Excitedly.)* Where? Have you found it?

Captain: No, no, no... *(Taking a deep breath.)* You're looking for a tropical island here in (name of place)?

Holidaymaker: *(Slightly impatiently.)* Yes! There must be a tropical island round here somewhere – look at all these bananas growing everywhere!

Captain: *(To audience.)* How many bananas can you see? Put your hand up when you have counted them all!

Holidaymaker: Bananas... That reminds me! I'm sure I've got a bit of paper here somewhere that says something about bananas! Let me see... Ah yes, here it is! *(Holding up an invitation with the **GOING BANANAS!** logo on the front.)* Hmmm... Going bananas... Going bananas? What does 'going bananas' mean?

Captain: *(To audience.)* Does anyone here know what 'going bananas' means? *(Either repeat the definition given, or explain as follows if no one knows.)* It means to go completely over the top about something – silly, crazy and... well... bananas!

Holidaymaker: Like me, you mean, looking for a tropical island in the middle of (name of place)?

Captain: *(Agreeing.)* Hmmmm!

Holidaymaker: I'm *sure* I've seen something about a tropical island though. Wait a minute! Yes! I was right! *(Opening the invitation.)*

Captain: What does it say?

Holidaymaker: It says... *(Reading out the invitation.)*

Captain: Hang on, hang on! Slow down! *What* does it say?

Holidaymaker: *(Repeating the information slowly and clearly.)*

Captain: So what sort of things will happen at **GOING BANANAS!**?

Holidaymaker: *(Talking enthusiastically about the programme, starting with the fact that it all happens on a tropical island where there will be games, singing, quizzes and an exciting story each day about someone in the Bible who went bananas. If they want to know what Mashed Bananas, Banana Splits, Bananaerobics and Banana-brains are, watch out for the Banana Piranha and meet the Banana Boys, they can come along and find out...)*

Captain: Tell you what, as everyone here is invited to **GOING BANANAS!**, why don't we give them an invitation each?

Holidaymaker: That's a brilliant idea! Now why didn't *I* think of that?

Captain: *(Explaining the procedure for distributing invitations.)* We'll look forward to seeing you all at **GOING BANANAS!** Bye!

PROMOTING GOING BANANAS!

It is no good running an airline if you do not have any passengers! Advertising **GOING BANANAS!** is a very important part of the advance preparations. If you forget it, you may find that Banana Island is deserted!

With your planning group, work out a promotion strategy suitable for your church and your locality. Appoint someone with the necessary skills and access to a computer to be responsible for all the publicity, posters, leaflet, banners, invitations and letters to the parents. This person could also keep your church updated with progress reports and current prayer needs.

18

POINTS TO CONSIDER

 ### Where will you target your recruiting?

If you can have access to local schools, they are a good place to start, as well as local organisations such as Brownies and Cubs. And don't forget the children who are already in the children's groups at your church.

 ### What will your publicity say?

Plan the wording carefully. Start with all the essential information such as dates and times, where it is happening, what age group it is aimed at and whether or not there are any charges. Make it sound exciting! Mention the Time Shed, Banana Splits, Bananaerobics, and so on. Make sure people who are interested know what to do next. For example, is it clear how they can obtain a registration form and what they should do with it once it is completed? Any leaflets, posters or banners should state that it is a Christian event with Bible teaching. **GOING BANANAS!** should be identified as a church-run activity, with a contact name and phone number printed on it.

 ### Is your artwork up to scratch?

All your publicity must be checked carefully for mistakes. Anything displayed or distributed should be well presented and look professional – scrappy, second-rate photocopies do not give a good impression. Make it visual and clear, but not too 'crowded'. Use the logo on everything – it helps! (The logo masters are on page 64.)

 ### How will you advertise GOING BANANAS!?

Arrange school assemblies and visit after-school clubs, football-coaching sessions, ballet classes and uniformed organisations. Simply give out invitations or use the sketch outlined on page 17. If you want to display posters, check before sticking them in shop windows or on lampposts. It is important to keep good relationships with local traders and the police. A leaflet drop can sometimes be effective, as well as word-of-mouth of course. Ready-made publicity material for your event can be obtained from CPO, Garcia Estate, Canterbury Road, Worthing, West Sussex, BN13 1BW.

SAMPLE LETTER TO PARENTS WITH A REGISTRATION FORM

(Note: This could be folded in half across the middle, with the logo photocopied on the outside.)

Who are the Banana Boys? What is Bananaerobics? When are Banana Splits? Where is Banana Island? Why Mashed Bananas? If you want to come and find out more, here is...

An invitation to GOING BANANAS!

Church logo and address
Contact phone number
Date

Dear Parent/Guardian

Would you like your child to be transported to a 'tropical island' at the end of the summer holidays (or whatever time of year you are running it)? Why not let them come along to (details of your venue) every morning (or afternoon) from.................... to...................... (dates), at................... until................ (times). We'll be **GOING BANANAS!** there and we'd love them to join us!

GOING BANANAS! is for 5-11 year olds (Reception to Year 6) and is being organised by members of (name of your church), completely free of charge (or state here what the charges are and what they cover, for example refreshments). It will be fast-moving and lots of fun with games, quizzes, zany presenters, a band, Bible stories and drama – all set on a tropical island!

If you would like your child to join us in **GOING BANANAS!** please complete the registration form below and return it by (date) at the latest. Space is limited, so places may have to be allocated on a first-come-first-served basis. Further information will be sent out nearer the time. If you have any queries, please contact (name) on (phone).

We are looking forward to seeing your child at **GOING BANANAS!**

Your Name

GOING BANANAS! Co-ordinator

Registration form for GOING BANANAS! (One per child, please)

Please tear off along the dotted line and return to...
....
.... (name and address of co-ordinator)

Full name of child.. Male/Female
Address...
Telephone number... Date of birth..Age...................
School...Class..................
Signed... (Parent/Guardian) Date...

SAMPLE PASSPORT (OUTSIDE COVER)

GOING BANANAS! Co-ordinator

Your Name

Please phone if you have any queries regarding this event.

at **GOING BANANAS!**

So that we can organise the children into groups and ensure their safety at all times, could you please complete the details overleaf? Once this passport has been returned, we'll be able to allocate your child a place

until .... (times). We're sure that all the children will have a good time!

to attend **GOING BANANAS!** in (details of your venue) from .... to .... (dates) at. ....

Thank you for returning the registration form for ....

Dear Parent/Guardian

Church logo and address
Contact phone number
Date

Fold along dotted lines

Name

_____

_____

Going BANANAS!

PASSPORT

SAMPLE PASSPORT (INSIDE SHEET)

(Note: The cover is printed on one side of the paper, with this inside page printed on the other side. The Passport is folded in half and in half again to A6 size. It will then all be the right way up, but check before you run off hundreds of copies!)

I give permission for my child to attend **GOING BANANAS!**

Full name ....

Address ....

Home telephone number ....

Date of birth .... Age ....

Telephone number where you can be contacted in an emergency ....

Name and telephone number of GP ....

Details of any known conditions, allergies, etc. (eg, asthma, diabetes)..........................

....

In the unlikely event of illness or accident, I give permission for any necessary medical treatment to be administered by the nominated first aider, or by suitably qualified medical practitioners. Should my child require emergency hospital treatment, I authorise an adult leader to sign on my behalf any written form of consent required by the hospital if I cannot be contacted. I understand that every effort will be made to contact me as soon as possible.

I confirm that the above details are correct to the best of my knowledge.

Signature .... (Parent/Guardian)

Date ....

Name of a friend attending **GOING BANANAS!** ....

My child will normally be collected by the following adult(s) at .... (time each session ends)

Name .... or ....

Please return this passport as soon as possible to

Your name
Contact address

We're looking forward to seeing your child at **GOING BANANAS!**

on (date) at (time)

PASSPORT CONTROL

Passport Control is a straightforward, efficient and fun way of organising the registration of children who come to your holiday club. It enables you to obtain essential information such as emergency telephone numbers and details of any medical conditions, and fits in with the theme of travelling to a tropical island. It operates as follows.

1 The invitations to **GOING BANANAS!** are in the form of a letter to parents which includes a tear-off registration form. An example of this is on page 19.
2 If a child wants to attend **GOING BANANAS!**, his or her parents must complete and return the form to the given address.
3 A Passport is then sent to the child with his or her name on it. An example of this is on pages 20 and 21.
4 Parents complete the permission form which is printed inside the Passport. This includes the details about their child that you need for safety and medical reasons.
5 The child brings the completed Passport with them the first time they attend **GOING BANANAS!**.

If you feel that the system is too complicated for your church, you could dispense with the initial registration form and send the Passport out with the letter of invitation. In this way, parents only have to complete and return one piece of paper, not two. However, the completed registration slip does act as a back-up if the Passport is lost. It also enables some advance planning to be done, such as allocating the Passengers to Banana Bunches, producing a master list for the people on the Departure Desks and getting a rough idea of how many children to expect on the first day.

6 However flustered they may feel, the team members organising Passport Control should be welcoming to the new, perhaps nervous Passengers and their parents. You will need at least three Departure Desks in the entrance area (small tables are fine), with an alphabetical label for each desk eg, 'A-G', 'H-R' and 'S-Z'. You will also need one person to staff the Enquiry Desk, which should be clearly labelled so that the Airport Staff at the door can direct any new arrivals without Passports, or children who just turn up, to that person.
7 As the Passengers arrive, at least one of the Airport Staff is waiting at the door and directs them to the correct Departure Desk, where they hand in their completed Passport.
8 Once their Passport has been stamped with the day's date and their Banana Bunch number has been written on it, the Passengers are told which Banana Bunch they are in. They can then say goodbye to their parents and go with another Airport Staff member to meet their Cabin Crew, and be introduced and warmly welcomed.
9 The Passports take the place of a register and are kept at Passport Control. Do not let the Passengers take them home as they may get lost. When **GOING BANANAS!** is over, the Passports will continue to be a valuable source of information for birthdays, names and addresses for follow-up. Each Departure Desk could have a shoe box as a filing system. When the Passengers arrive each day and give their name, stamp their Passport so that you know they are present (eg, in case of fire) and file it.
10 As soon as all the Passengers have been through Passport Control, turn the Departure Desks around, ready for Disembarkation. At Disembarkation, the Passengers go to their desk where Passport Control and Airport Staff will let them leave only when they have identified the adult who is collecting them.

Equipment needed

Each Departure Desk should be equipped with:
* a chair
* the appropriate alphabetical notice
* a pen
* a date stamp and ink pad
* a shoe box for filing the Passports

The Enquiry Desk will need:
* Spare Passports and pens for new arrivals without Passports, or for the re-issue of lost Passports
* A master list of all those who have booked in so far, so that maximum numbers are not exceeded

DAY 1 Noah

TEAM TIME

9.00

The team arrives, wearing **GOING BANANAS!** t-shirts (if available) and name badges so that children and parents will know who they are.

Welcome everyone. Go straight into a Bible focus and a short time of prayer.

Read Psalm 52 together, pointing out the parts that show how much God loves people and those which are about his judgment.

Ask team members to praise God for who he is and what he is like, and to pray that the children will begin to understand that there are two ways to live – believing and trusting in God, or rejecting him. The team could either call out one-sentence prayers, or pray silently.

Go through the answers to the Big Questions that everyone will discuss in Banana Bunches today.

BIG QUESTIONS

Bible passage
Genesis 6:9-22

Who is God?
Lord of all creation and history.

What is he like?
He is the Creator, is saddened by sin, judges, loves, and makes promises he keeps.

Who 'went bananas' and why?
Noah. He built a boat in the middle of the country when there was no water and no sign of rain. He did it because God told him to.

What did God do?
He wiped out all creation apart from Noah, his family and the animals. He made a new start with creation (though there was still sin), and promised not to flood the earth again.

What doesn't God want?
Evil, violence, arrogance, sin and people living without him.

What does he want?
Faith, 'righteousness', obedience and 'fellowship'.

9.15

Brief the team, with a quick run-through of the day's programme including instructions for making Cool Shades and playing The Creation Game. Explain Banana Skins and Mashed Bananas for the team's benefit.

9.25

Passport Control and the Cabin Crew get into position. Noah squeezes into the Time Shed, ready for his dramatic entrance and interview later. The Banana Boys take up their positions ready to get on stage once the lights are dimmed for take-off. The Banana Band is ready to strike up.

Bananas Wired for Sound and Light have cued the sound effects.

Equipment needed

Banana Boys
* Copy of the day's programme
* Song words on overhead projector acetates
* Whistle
* Several pairs of swimming trunks
* Banana Bin placed on a table at the side
* Pencils and yellow paper cut into banana shapes

Cabin Crew
* Name badges

For Banana Bunches 1 each Banana Bunch will need:
* Photocopies of Cool Shades from the master on page 29, enough for one each
* Felt-tip pens * Crayons
* Pencils * Scissors
* Stapler with staples (for adults to use, not the children)
* Reel of sticky tape

For Banana Bunches 2 each Banana Bunch will need:
* The Creation Game instructions copied from the master on page 30 (two copies if you have a large group, so that you can split into two smaller groups)
* 1 small mirror
* 2 balloons (one spare in case the first one pops!)

For Banana Bunches 3 each Banana Bunch will need:
* Blank speech bubble sheets
* Postcards Home from the master on page 31 (enough for one each)
* Felt-tip pens
* Crayons
* Pencils

For Banana Skins each Banana Bunch will need:
* 1 yellow toilet roll

PROGRAMME AT A GLANCE

9.00
Team arrives for Bible focus and prayer

9.15
Team briefing

9.25
Into positions

Banana Bunches 1

Fun background music playing quietly

10.00
GOING BANANAS! song

10.05
Welcome/flight sequence/sound effects

10.10
Banana Boys 1

10.20
Songs 1 and 2

10.32
Banana Bunches 2

10.45
Banana Boys 2

The Time Shed Interview

10.53
Whistle for Banana Skins

10.58
Banana Splits

Fun background music playing quietly

11.10
Mashed Bananas

11.20
Song

11.25
Video Story 1

Talk Time

11.32
Banana Bunches 3

11.50
Prayer

11.53
Return flight sequence/ sound effects

11.58
GOING BANANAS! song

12.00
Disembarkation

12.15
Team de-briefing and prayer

PROGRAMME IN DETAIL

BIBLE PASSAGE Genesis 6:9-22

KEY BIBLE VERSE Deuteronomy 6:5

9.30

Everyone is ready for early arrivals. Quiet background music is playing. Passport Control begins checking in the first Passengers by stamping their Passports. The Airport Staff welcome Passengers and take them to meet their Cabin Crew members, who introduce themselves, give each Passenger a badge with their name on and explain how to make Cool Shades.

BANANA BUNCHES 1:
MAKING GOING BANANAS! COOL SHADES

This is an introductory fun activity which acts as an icebreaker. Give each child one piece of thin card with the Cool Shades outline on it copied from the master on page 29. They design their own, colour them in and cut them out, with help if necessary. They then need to cut out the strip printed at the side of the card. This goes around the back of their head to hold the shades on. It is attached to either side of the shades with a staple, which is then covered in sticky tape for added strength and protection. (From the front the Cool Shades resemble sun-glasses, but at the back they look like a headband.) Older Passengers may be able to help each other with this, but an adult should assist the younger ones. They will all need help to cut out the eye holes – do make sure your scissors have rounded ends. Remember to write the child's name on his or her pair of Cool Shades.

9.55

The Banana Band starts playing fun background music. The Cabin Crew clear up the Cool Shades, bits of card, scissors and other materials.

10.00

The Banana Band perform then teach the **GOING BANANAS!** song.

10.05

The Captain welcomes passengers on board in a traditional 'This is your Captain speaking' style, using or adapting the script on page 17. He explains the rules, the location of toilets, fire exits and other practical necessities. An assistant could go through a fun, stereotypical safety routine at this point, including a few manic actions with which the Passengers can join in. Bananas Wired for Sound and Light dim the lights, close the blinds or curtains, switch on the runway lights (Christmas tree lights round the edge of the room) and then play the sound effect of a 747 taking off. This is followed by sound effects of waves and seagulls, which fade out when the Banana Boys appear.

10.10

The Captain welcomes the Passengers to Banana Island and warns them about the Banana Boys – one is lazy, the other is bossy and their bananas are always bad because they never get them picked in time! The Banana Boys (Ripe and Rotten) are already sitting in their deck-chairs, but leap up and take over as presenters.

From this point the Banana Boys use Script 1 from page 26.

10.15

Ripe introduces the Cabin Crew and the Airport Staff, and warns of Banana Skins to come – a quick-fire activity, identified by a whistle, which may come at any point in the programme. The first Banana Skins involves creating a human banana in only four minutes by 'mummifying' a group member with one yellow toilet roll.

Rotten explains that any volunteers for Mashed Bananas need to write their names on a paper banana and post it in the Banana Bin during the Banana Splits refreshment break.

10.20

Rotten introduces and leads a couple of songs.

Then Ripe introduces The Creation Game.

10.32 *Go & change into Time Machine.*

BANANA BUNCHES 2: THE CREATION GAME

This activity sets the scene for the Bible story. Spread out the Banana Bunches as much as possible to play The Creation Game. The master for this game is printed on page 30.

10.42

Ripe concludes, 'Everything seemed to be perfect. Then people thought they knew better than God and things got worse and worse and worse... '

10.45

The Banana Boys introduce the Time Shed. They use Script 2 here from page 27.

Cue Bananas Wired for Sound and Light for the time-travel sound effects and lighting.

10.48

THE TIME SHED INTERVIEW

Everyone meets Noah. The Banana Boys interview him to find out what he did. Ripe asks over-serious questions, Rotten over-silly questions, then their questions and comments converge to make the point.

10.52

The Time Shed procedure operates in reverse, with sounds, actions and lighting.

10.53

Rotten blows the whistle for Banana Skins.

10.58

Ripe judges the best human bananas briefly, then announces Banana Splits (refreshments). Everyone should stay sitting in their Banana Bunches.

11.00

The Banana Splits team serve refreshments to Banana Bunches in their places. This is the opportunity for Passengers and any team members to write their names on slips of paper to volunteer for Mashed Bananas. They put them in the Banana Bin. Passengers also have a little time now to finish making their Cool Shades. The Banana Band plays fun, background music.

11.10

Ripe welcomes everyone back and admires the Cool Shades. The Banana Boys pick names out of the Banana Bin to provide contestants for Mashed Bananas – The Terrible Swimming Trunk Tangle. They could organise this in heats if necessary, using several pairs of old swimming trunks. Each contestant needs an adult behind them to keep his or her score. Contestants have forty-five seconds to see how many times they can step into the trunks, pull them up over their knees and then step out of them again.

11.20

Rotten introduces and leads a song.

11.25

Story 1 of the **GOING BANANAS!** video, followed by Talk Time with the Navigator, using the outline on page 28.

11.32

BANANA BUNCHES 3: BIG QUESTIONS

This is a chance for the Passengers to respond to the teaching. They and their Cabin Crew discuss the Big Questions. Cabin Crew members invite Passengers to write or draw the group's agreed answers on the speech bubbles. Finally the Passengers write their Postcards Home. The master for these is printed on page 31. Younger children may need help.

11.50

The Captain gets everyone together again and leads a simple, brief prayer from the front, explaining that shutting our eyes and keeping our hands together can help us to concentrate and remember who we are talking to – the great God and Creator we have learnt about today.

11.53

Then the Captain talks everyone through the flight home.

11.55

Bananas Wired for Sound and Light use the same sound effects as before except this time, of course, the 747 is landing. The Captain talks the plane down.

11.58

The Banana Band introduces and leads the **GOING BANANAS!** song for the last time.

12.00

The Captain explains Disembarkation. Passengers cannot go until they are told to – one Banana Bunch at a time. They must hand their badge to their Cabin Crew before they leave, so that they can have it when they next come to **GOING BANANAS!**. When all this has been made clear, the Captain dismisses the Passengers one Banana Bunch at a time. 'See you tomorrow!' The Banana Band plays fun, background music as everyone leaves, or a reprieve of some of the songs which have been sung during the event.

12.15

The whole team stays for the de-briefing session and a welcome cup of tea or coffee provided by Banana Splits. This is an opportunity to chat about the session, and to get valuable feedback about things in the programme which did or did not work, so that any necessary changes can be made. The team could pray together, focusing on individual children with specific needs.

BANANA BOYS SCRIPT 1

Ripe: Hello! My name's Ripe.
Rotten: And I'm Rotten.
Ripe: *(Sniggering.)* And we're the Banana Boys. We'd better say hello to the boys. Hello to the boys! *(He waits for the boys to respond and repeats it in pantomime style once or twice to get a better response.)* And hello to the girls! *(Same as before.)*
Rotten: Welcome to Banana Island!
Ripe: There are a lot of exciting things to do here, but first there's something you need to know.
Rotten: What's that?
Ripe: You *know* what!
Rotten: You know what what? *(Ripe whispers to Rotten.)* Oh yeah, of course!
Ripe: There's something you need to shout.
Rotten: Every time you hear us say, 'If you're happy or you're sad, if you're gloomy or you're glad...'
Ripe: You shout back, 'Let's all go bananas!'
Rotten: Do you think you've got that? Let's give it a go! If you're happy or you're sad...

Ripe: If you're gloomy or you're glad...
All: Let's all go bananas!
(Ripe and Rotten repeat this once or twice to practise.)
Ripe: There's one more thing you need to know. Every time someone says, 'Listen up!' you shout 'OK!', put both thumbs up then keep quiet because it means that someone wants to tell you something important. *(Practise this once only.)*
Ripe: So what do you think we should do with all our visitors today, Rotten?
Rotten: Dunno. But I know what *I'm* going to do.
Ripe: What's that then?
Rotten: Same as usual.
Ripe: Yeah, well, what's *that* then?
Rotten: I'm going to sit in this deck-chair and have a rest. *(He sits down, puts his hat over his eyes and goes to sleep, snoring loudly.)*

Ripe: *(To the Passengers.)* Rotten's so lazy. He never wants to get out there picking bananas. I'll have to think of a way to get him out of that chair... Hmmm. Maybe some singing will help my brain to work. That's what we're going to do now. *(Introduces songs.)*

BANANA BOYS SCRIPT 2 WITH THE TIME SHED INTERVIEW

Rotten: You know what?
Ripe: What?
Rotten: I like it here but we need some adventure.
Ripe: Well, picking bananas is quite exciting. You should try it some time!
Rotten: Hey, do you remember that funny bloke who came round the island a couple of years ago?
Ripe: Yeah, he was trying to sell something, wasn't he?
Rotten: We gave him a load of bananas and he let us use a thing he called... a Time Shed.
Ripe: That's right. He said we could use it for one week every year for free.
Rotten: Yeah, it was a time-share Time Shed! I've got a piece of paper here that tells us which week we can use it. *(He produces a tatty piece of paper from his pocket.)*
Ripe: Give it here. Let me see it. *(He snatches the paper from Rotten and looks at it.)* It says the (whichever week your holiday club is running)!
Rotten: Hey, wait a minute! That's now!
Ripe: I wonder where that Time Shed went.
Rotten: Easy question. It's that shed over there that we keep our tools in.
Ripe: Do you think we should try to get it to work?
Rotten: Yeah, may as well. You haven't succeeded with *me* though, have you? But... err... don't you think it's a bit scary?
Ripe: *I'm* not scared.
Rotten: Oh yes you are!
Ripe: Oh no I'm not! *(Continued in pantomime style involving the children.)* Now where are the instructions to make it work?
Rotten: Look! They're on the back of

the paper. It says, 'Get (number present) children to shout out the special countdown.' Where will we find (number) children?
Ripe: *(To the Passengers.)* Any ideas?
Rotten: OK. Will *you* lot help us count down?
All: Ten, nine, eight, seven, six, five, four, three, two, one, zero...
(The Time Shed bursts into action. Noah falls out of the Time Shed door coughing and shaken.)
Ripe: Hello. Who are you?
Noah: Noah.
Ripe: Noah who?
Rotten: Know a man who wants to buy a car?
Noah: No. Just Noah.
Rotten: Oh, *that* Noah! *(To Ripe.)* You know-a, that Noah! *(To Noah.)* You don't want to buy a second-hand Escort, do you?
Noah: No, I don't think so... whatever a second-hand Escort is.
Rotten: But *you're* in the travel business, aren't you?
Noah: In a way, yes. In fact, I was working on my own boat just now when there was this rushing sound and next thing I knew, I was inside your... err... shed... thing.
Rotten: Yeah, groovy, innit?!
Noah: But who are you two?
Rotten: Mind yer own boat-building business!
Ripe: Sssh!... Don't be so rude!... Umm, my name's Ripe and this is Rotten.
Noah: Yes, I *thought* I smelt something peculiar around here.
Rotten: Oi, mush! We do the jokes!
Ripe: We're the Banana Boys and this is **GOING BANANAS!**
Rotten: If you're happy or you're sad...
Ripe: If you're gloomy or you're glad...
All: Let's all go bananas!
Noah: *(Chuckles.)* Oh yes, that fits. *That's* why I'm here. People thought *I'd* gone bananas when they saw me building my boat in the middle of dry land. There was no sign of rain... or river or sea or ocean at all! Hah!
Rotten: So why *were* you building it?

Noah: *God* told me to.
Rotten: Fair enough... *(He does a double take.)* Who told you to?
Noah: The God of all creation. He told me how sad he was at the wrong that people were doing all over the world, and said he wanted to flood the lot and start again.
Ripe: Wow!
Rotten: Wow again!
Noah: He also told me that me and the missus, our sons and their wives will survive in the boat... Oh yes, and so will the animals!
Rotten: You've got a dog? What's his name?
Noah: Well, I *will* have a dog. Two, in fact. *(He takes out a long list that unrolls.)* And some horses, monkeys, camels, cats, chickens, cows, bears, foxes, lions and...
Rotten: And some fleas, I expect!
Noah: *(Missing the joke.)* Oh yes, I should think so... somewhere here.
Rotten: Won't the neighbours complain with all that row going on?
Noah: I'm afraid there won't be any neighbours.
Rotten: *(Sadly, realizing what he has said.)* Err, yes... you *said*.
Noah: All the animals will be in the boat with us.
Rotten: *(Holding his nose.)* Pooh!
Ripe: But isn't all this a bit mean of God?
Rotten: What, you mean making them all go in the boat with *him*? *(Indicating Noah with his thumb.)*
Noah: *(Ignoring Rotten.)* He's a God who hates evil and wrong, and won't put up with it for ever. But he's also a God who loves all he has made so much that he'll make a new start... when the rain stops. And he'll never give up on us. *(Holding his palm out.)* Oh, I can feel a spot now... Look, can you get me back where I belong? I'll just get the roof done in time by the look of it.
(Noah enters the Time Shed. Routine.)

* TALK TIME * TALK TIME * TALK TIME *

(Look round, peering into the Time Shed.) It's a pity Noah has gone. I wanted to ask him a few more questions. Never mind. We'll find out more about him from the Bible. *(Hold up a Good News Bible.)* Right at the start in fact. Noah's story comes in the Bible book called Genesis. Genesis means beginnings.

And that's what it was all about – the beginning, the new start God made with Noah. In The Creation Game, we discovered that God made everything at the very beginning. *(Read Genesis 1:1.)* How did he feel when it was all finished? Let's find out. *(Read Genesis 1:10,12,18 and 31, quoting '... and God was pleased' each time.)* He was pleased!

(Display an overhead projector acetate picture of the world, which could be copied simply from an atlas.) But, unfortunately, God's world was spoilt. *(Scribble roughly all over the acetate, obviously spoiling it.)* Why? Why did it all go wrong? It was people. People like you and me, who began to change. They stopped going God's way and started to go their own way. They didn't take notice of God any more. They hurt each other and they hurt God. He *wasn't* pleased.

The Bible calls this wrong way 'sin'. It's when we put ourselves first. What is the middle letter in the word 'sin'? *(Write the word 'sin' with a **washable** overhead projector pen on a clean acetate.)* That's what it's all about. It's when we say, '*I* don't care!' or '*I* don't want to take any notice of what God wants!' 'I, I, I... ' This is what the Bible

tells us. *(Read Genesis 6:5-7.)* That's one of the saddest parts of the Bible. God loves us very, very much. But there's no messing about with him. He hates the wrong things we do, the wrong things we say and the wrong things we think. He wants to get rid of all the evil, selfishness and violence in the world. *(As you say each of these three words, use the **washable** pen and write them around the word 'sin' on the acetate.)*

But... wait a minute! Phew! *(Read Genesis 6:8, then pause.)* Listen to what God told Noah. *(Read Genesis 6:10-14,17-22.)* Everyone thought Noah had gone bananas, but what he did made sense because... *(Read Genesis 7:23-24, then draw a simple ark on the acetate with a **permanent** overhead projector pen.)*

(Now, slowly and carefully, get the wet cloth, squeeze out most of the water and then, very gently, let a few drops drip onto the acetate, so that it looks like rain. Be careful it does not drip into the electrics! To finish the effect, wipe the words off the acetate so that it is completely clean, apart from the ark. It should speak for itself!)

God made a new start and because Noah was his friend, God saved him. God wants us to be like Noah and to be his friends. And that's what **GOING BANANAS!** is all about – finding out more about being God's friend.

Now it's time for Banana Bunches again. This time, see how much of the story of Noah you can remember. Your Cabin Crew will tell you what to do.

* TALK TIME * TALK TIME * TALK TIME *

COOL SHADES

Welcome to
GOING BANANAS!

Can you decorate your
Cool Shades to make
them look really cool?
When they are coloured
in, cut them out around
the outline. Then, very
slowly and carefully, cut
out the eye holes in the
middle. Next, cut the
strip from the side and
ask your Cabin Crew to
help you join end A to A
and B to B, using a
stapler and sticky
tape. Then your Cool
Shades will fit well and
will not slip down over
your eyes!

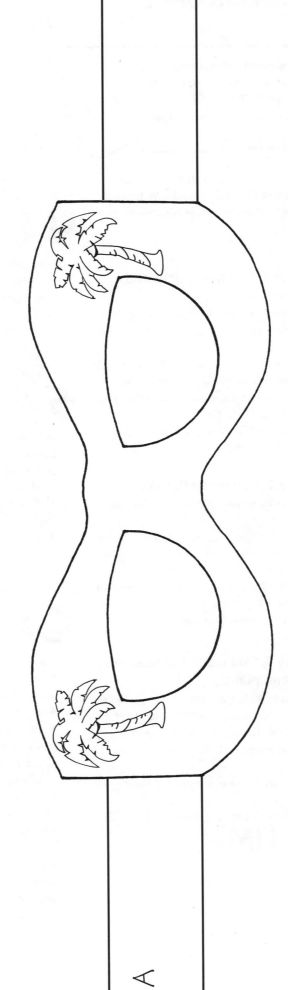

THE CREATION GAME

The Bible tells us that God created everything in six days, and rested on the seventh. We have six tasks to do to help us remember what he made on which day.

On Day 1, God made light and darkness.

- As soon as I have finished reading these instructions, everyone must shut their eyes tightly.
- I shall count down 10, 9, 8, 7, 6, 5, 4, 3, 2, 1. Everyone must then open their eyes as quickly as they can and shout out the name of the first person or thing they see.
- Then we must all say, 'Wow! God made it!'
- Do it and then shout, 'Wow! God made it!'
- Shut your eyes! 10, 9, ... etc.

On Day 2, God made the sky.

- One person must blow up a balloon and tie a knot in it.
- By hitting it among us, we have to keep the balloon 'up in the sky' for thirty seconds. One Cabin Crew member will time us.
- When we have completed thirty seconds, we must all shout, 'Wow! God made it!'
- Do it and then shout, 'Wow! God made it!'

On Day 3, God made the land, sea, trees and plants.

- Giant sequoia trees grow up to 7.6 metres across – wide enough to drive a car through their trunk. That's about as wide as eight of you standing in a line, arms outstretched with fingers touching.
- When those eight are in place, we must all shout, 'Wow! God made it!'
- Do it and then shout, 'Wow! God made it!'

On Day 4, God made the sun, moon, stars, days, months and years.

- Everyone in our Banana Bunch must line up in order, starting with the oldest first, the youngest last, and everyone else in place in between.
- When everyone is in place, we must all shout, 'Wow! God made it!'
- Do it and then shout, 'Wow! God made it!'

On Day 5, God created sea creatures and birds.

- The male African ostrich is the largest bird. It grows to a height of 2.5 metres. Without writing or sticking anything on a wall, we must measure this height against a wall and get our tallest Cabin Crew member to put a finger at the top of the 'ostrich'. Down the side of this sheet is a line 25 centimetres long, to help us.
- When it's measured, we must all shout, 'Wow! God made it!'
- Do it and then shout, 'Wow! God made it!'

On Day 6, God created land animals and people.

- The anaconda and the python are the longest snakes. Both grow up to 9 metres long. That's six of us lying on the floor in a line head to toe, wriggling.
- When the snake is finished and wriggling, we must all shout, 'Wow! God made it!'
- Do it and then shout, 'Wow! God made it!'
- But the best bit of God's creation was still to come. Everyone must stand in a circle. One Cabin Crew member will come round for everyone to look at themselves in the mirror.
- When we have all had a look, we must all shout, 'Wow! God made me!'
- Do it and then shout, 'Wow! God made me!'

When we have finished all six tasks, we must sit down and try to remember together the order in which God created everything. When we think we've got it, we must lie on our backs and rest. Finished!

POSTCARD HOME

_____

_____

_____

_____

Going Bananas

Dear

Today I went to GOING BANANAS!

It was ☐ OK ☐ brilliant
☐ nice and noisy ☐ rubbish.

There were a lot of
☐ fun things to do ☐ bananas
☐ sweaty people around.

I had ☐ a nasty accident with a banana
☐ a drink
☐ my name down for The Terrible Swimming Trunk Tangle.

We learnt that Noah went bananas and built a boat on dry land. The best thing I discovered about God was that......................

Lots of love from

NOAH

Find out what the Bible says about Noah.

✱ Start at the arrow and follow the line.
✱ Write down the letters in the right order.
✱ Divide up the words so that it all makes sense.

....

....

DAY 2 Gideon

TEAM TIME

9.00

The team arrives, wearing their badges and t-shirts.

Have a very brief feedback on the first day and then move on to the Bible focus. Read 2 Corinthians 12:9 together and remind the team how we all feel weak and vulnerable at different times and about different things, but perhaps especially at the moment about our role in **GOING BANANAS!** Paul reminds us that God uses our weakness to demonstrate his power, just as he did with Paul himself, and also of course with Gideon.

Have a time of prayer, all together, in small groups or in pairs. Ask the team to pray for an openness to God, so that he will be able to work through them. At the end of the prayer time, read these verses of encouragement: Joshua 1:9, Matthew 28:20, John 14:16-17 and Hebrews 13:6.

Go through the answers to the Big Questions that everyone will discuss in Banana Bunches today.

BIG QUESTIONS

Bible Passage
Judges 6,7

Who is God?
The King of his people.

What is he like?
He rescues, keeps his promises, sends people on missions, is present with his people, does miraculous things, brings peace, speaks to his people and is powerful.

Who 'went bananas' and why?
Gideon. Just when he needed the strongest possible army, he knocked it back to 300 men, because God told him to. God wanted to show his power.

What did God do?
He used someone as 'insignificant' as Gideon to help make his people Israel safe and strong.

What doesn't God want?
People who worship anyone or anything but him, people to think he is weak and his people to reckon they don't need him.

What does he want?
Trust in his promises, brave living, knowledge of who we are in his sight, and recognition that he is the only true God.

9.15

Brief the team with a run-through of the day's programme, including instructions for Monkeying About and The Great Bread Roll. Mention Message in a Bottle and Bananaerobics so that the team are prepared.

9.25

Passport Control, Cabin Crew and the Banana Band move into position, with Gideon already concealed in the Time Shed.

Equipment needed

Banana Boys
* Copy of the day's programme
* Song words on overhead projector acetates
* A water pistol and a bucket of water
* Message in a Bottle and paper and pencils ready
* Workout tape for Bananaerobics
* Good News Bible

Cabin Crew
* Name badges

For Banana Bunches 1 each Banana Bunch will need:
* Several copies of the Monkeying About game

(master on page 38) for the Passengers to play in small groups
* Plenty of counters and dice

For Banana Bunches 2 each Banana Bunch will need:
* A ball (a football is best) for The Great Bread Roll

For Banana Bunches 3 each Banana Bunch will need:
* Blank speech bubble sheets
* Postcards Home (enough copies for one each from the master on page 39)
* Felt-tip pens
* Crayons
* Pencils

PROGRAMME AT A GLANCE

9.00 Team arrives for Bible focus and prayer

9.15 Team briefing

9.25 Into positions
Banana Bunches 1
Fun background music playing quietly

10.00 GOING BANANAS! song twice

10.07 Welcome/flight sequence/sound effects

10.10 Banana Boys 1

10.20 Songs 1 and 2

10.30 Explanation of Message in a Bottle

10.35 GOING BANANAS! shout
Bananaerobics

10.45 Video Story 2

10.55 The Time Shed Interview

11.00 Banana Bunches 2

11.10 Banana Splits
Fun background music playing quietly

11.20 Song 3

11.25 Talk Time
Prayer

11.32 Banana Bunches 3

11.55 Message in a Bottle
Return flight sequence/sound effects

11.58 GOING BANANAS! song

12.00 Disembarkation

12.15 Team de-briefing and prayer

PROGRAMME IN DETAIL

BIBLE PASSAGE Judges 6,7

KEY BIBLE VERSE 2 Corinthians 12:9

9.30

Everyone should be ready and in position, with Passport Control and Banana Bunches prepared for new arrivals today – word may have got around after the first session! The Banana Band plays fun background music. As the Passengers arrive, give them their badge, or get them to find it themselves (a good chance to remind yourself of their name!). Welcome them and invite them to join in with the Monkeying About game.

BANANA BUNCHES 1: MONKEYING ABOUT

This is a simple board game using copies of the game (from the master on page 38) and enough counters and dice for several games per Banana Bunch. There are simple questions to be answered if a player lands on certain squares, as well as some light-hearted forfeits which can be chosen and delegated. The idea is that it will help the Banana Bunches to get to know each other. Passengers can join in with it as they arrive and could play in pairs if they are new or shy. Give them a counter and explain that they can choose their forfeit and ask someone to do their forfeit for them if they want to.The forfeits are not meant to be threatening – it is important not to make anyone feel stupid. However, Cabin Crew and Airport Staff must be prepared to 'monkey around' if they do a forfeit. Banana Bunches can split into smaller groups for this game, so there may be several groups playing, but make sure there is a Cabin Crew or Airport Staff member with each one.

10.00

The Banana Band lead the **GOING BANANAS!** song twice.

10.07

The Captain welcomes passengers on board, explains the rules about keeping away from the stage and band area for safety reasons, reminds everyone of the location and use of the toilets (only at Banana Split time unless an absolute emergency!) and indicates the fire exits. The Captain leads into same procedure as Day 1 for take-off using the script on page 17, with an assistant doing a spoof routine if appropriate.

This is followed by sound effects of an aeroplane taking off. As the plane lands, seagull and wave noises, as for Day 1.

10.10

The Captain welcomes the Passengers to Banana Island and tell them to watch out for the Banana Boys.

The Banana Boys take over as presenters.

The Banana Boys use their rehearsed ad lib here, with Script 1 on page 35 as a guideline.

10.20

The Banana Boys introduce the bafflingly brilliant Banana Band and lead two songs. Re-cap on one from yesterday and teach a new one.

10.30

Ripe explains Message in a Bottle. During Banana Splits anyone (Passengers or Cabin Crew) can write a message to put in the bottle, which will be at the front of the stage. It could be a short prayer of thanks about something they have enjoyed at **GOING BANANAS!** or a letter to the Banana Boys, a question they may have, a riddle or suitable joke. No one has to put their name on the paper, and spelling and writing do not matter. Alternatively, the Passengers could write a message at home and put it in the bottle the following day.

Towards the end of the **GOING BANANAS!** session, when Ripe and Rotten are not around, one of the Banana Band chooses a Passenger to throw the bottle into the 'sea', hoping that the Banana Boys will find it the next day. Next day, the Banana Boys 'discover' the bottle floating in the 'sea' and choose a volunteer to fish it out with the net. They cut it open and read out the messages. The Captain could read out any prayers at the end of the session. If there are difficult theological questions which need to be answered, keep them back. Towards the end of the week you may want to ask your church leader to make a guest appearance to answer them.

10.35

Rotten does the **GOING BANANAS!** shout and introduces Bananaerobics. This is a gentle workout routine to music for three or four minutes, led from the front by Ripe and Rotten. (If it is not their thing, they could ask a willing team member to lead it – there must be someone who enjoys aerobics!) Having let off steam, the Passengers should be ready to concentrate on the video.

10.45

Story 2 of the **GOING BANANAS!** video.

10.55

Bananas Wired for Sound and Light do the sound effects (at which point the Banana Boys appear) and lighting for the Time Shed Interview.

10.56

THE TIME SHED INTERVIEW

Ripe and Rotten interview Gideon.

11.00

BANANA BUNCHES 2: THE GREAT BREAD ROLL

The Banana Boys introduce Banana Bunches 2: The Great Bread Roll. Ripe asks the Navigator to remind everyone how God used a dream to help Gideon trust him. The Navigator reads Judges 7:9-15 from the Good News Bible. Rotten explains the game, using one Banana Bunch team to demonstrate to everyone else how it is played. The Banana Bunch forms a long line, one in front of another, standing with legs apart to form a long tunnel or, for the purposes of this game, a tent! The person at the front has the ball, which represents the great bread roll from the dream. On a given signal, the 'bread' is rolled down through the 'tent', helped on its way if necessary. The person at the back catches it and runs to the front, when the procedure starts again! The game continues until everyone has had a turn and the leader is back at the front. As they finish, each Banana Bunch must sit down, still in their line. To make the game fair, there may need to be a bit of juggling with numbers if the Banana Bunches vary in size.

11.10

Banana Splits serve refreshments to the Banana Bunches, as before. The Banana Boys remind the Passengers that this is an opportunity for them to go to the toilet, finish their glasses from yesterday and write a message for Message in a Bottle if they want to. The Banana Band plays fun, background music.

11.20

The Banana Boys welcome everyone back and introduce and lead a song.

11.25

The Navigator does Talk Time, using the outline on page 37. The Navigator finishes with a prayer, based on the key verse 2 Corinthians 12:9 ('... my power is greatest when you are weak') asking God to help us remember that he will help us when we feel weak, perhaps when we are at school. Then the Navigator introduces Big Questions.

11.32

BANANA BUNCHES 3: BIG QUESTIONS

The Banana Bunches have a chance to respond to all the different elements of today's Bible story when they discuss the Big Questions with their Cabin Crew. Then they complete the speech bubbles, followed by their Postcards Home (from the master on page 39).

11.55

The Captain gets everyone together again. One of the Banana Band is asked to choose a Passenger to throw the Message in a Bottle into the 'sea' at the back of the stage. Then the Captain talks everyone through the return flight (using the script on page 17). Bananas Wired for Sound and Light do the sound effects and lighting.

11.58

The Banana Band introduces and leads the **GOING BANANAS!** song for the last time today.

12.00

The Captain announces Disembarkation, and asks the Cabin Crew to collect all their Passengers' badges before they go. The Captain dismisses the Passengers one Banana Bunch at a time. The Banana Band plays fun, background music as everyone leaves.

12.15

The team meets to de-brief and pray.

BANANA BOYS SCRIPT 1

(For this sketch, Ripe needs a water pistol and a bucket of water. Rotten enters full of energy, jumps up and down in keep-fit style, does press-ups, running on the spot and so on. Ripe follows holding the water pistol. He looks bemused by Rotten's behaviour.)

Rotten: Good morning, good morning, good morning! Good morning to the boys! *(Waits for reply.)* Good morning to the girls! *(Waits.)* What a wonderful morning this is! *(Sings.)* 'Oh what a beautiful morning, oh what a beautiful day...'

Ripe: *(Interrupts.)* Rotten?

Rotten: That's me!

Ripe: Er... are you all right?

Rotten: Never been better!

Ripe: That's what I'm worried about. *(To audience.)* I think he's gone bananas!

*(Rotten starts **GOING BANANAS!** shout. Ripe joins in.)*

Ripe: Rotten, do you think you ought to sit down? Maybe you've been overdoing it lately, although I can't imagine how. Why not come and take the weight off your brain... er... your feet? Have a rest.

Rotten: Oh no! Life's much too short for sleeping! There's work to be done.

Ripe: Well yes, there is. *(Indicates water pistol.)* I'm about to water the banana trees. But I'm worried about you, you're not usually so... *(Interrupts himself.)* That's it! Sleeping! Rotten isn't awake – he's sleep-walking! That explains it! Now how can we wake him up? Hmmm... he could do with a shock of some sort. Something cold maybe... *(To audience.)* Anyone here got any ideas? *(Waves water pistol around obliviously, inviting the obvious suggestion from the audience.)* Wow! What a brilliant idea! *(At this point Ripe could invite a Passenger to come and squirt Rotten with the water pistol. Once squirted, Rotten 'wakes up' dramatically.)*

Rotten: Uh? What's happening? Where am I? Why aren't I sitting in my deck-chair? *(Staggers over to deck-chair, sits down and falls asleep.)*

Ripe: *(Dismayed.)* Oh no! Rotten! Wake up! It's time to do some singing with the Banana Band.

Rotten: *(Jumps up and grins.)* Now you're talking! *(Surprised and innocent.)* You didn't think I was asleep did you? What are we singing then? *(Ripe introduces songs.)*

BANANA BOYS SCRIPT 2 WITH THE TIME SHED INTERVIEW

Gideon: *(Bursting exitedly out of Time Shed.)* We won!

Ripe: *(Punching his fist in the air.)* Yeah!

Rotten: He won! *(Chanting and clapping three times, in football style.)*

Ripe and **Rotten:** *(Together.)* He won! *(Clap x 3.)* He won! *(Clap x 3.)*

Ripe: Won what?

Rotten: One-nil of course!

Gideon: Eh?

Rotten: *(Impatiently.)* What was the score?

Gideon: Score?

Ripe: *(Patiently.)* The match you've just won. What was the score?

Gideon: Ah well, it wasn't really a match. It was a *battle!*

Rotten: *(Sounding surprised.)* What, you mean the crowd on the pitch?

Gideon: No, against the Midianites.

Rotten: Funny time to have a battle – middle of the night!

Ripe: No! Not the middle of the night, you fool – the *Midianites!*

Rotten: Oh yeah... Who are they?

Gideon: They are... errr... were a very large, very strong, very powerful, very tough army. They've been bossing the Israelites around. There are... errr... *were* thousands of them!

Rotten: *(Confidently.)* But you beat them!

Gideon: Yes, we did!

Rotten: Well, your army must be huge and really, really, *really* strong and...

Gideon: *(Interrupting.)* Oh no.

Ripe: No?

Gideon: Well... I did have 32,000 men, but I got rid of a load of them. So in the end it was... well... *small.*

Ripe: It was? When you say small, you still had more than they did. What are we talking here? 20,000? 10,000?

Gideon: No. 300.

Ripe and **Rotten:** *(Together, in a squeak.)* 300?

Rotten: How come?

Gideon: Because God told me to.

Ripe: Oh! That's OK then.

Rotten: I dunno. It sounds bananas to me.

Gideon: Well, God wanted us to trust *him* and not to think we could do it ourselves.

Ripe: But weren't you scared silly?

Gideon: No, not really. You see, I knew God was on our side, so we were going to win.

Rotten: *(Curious.)* How did you know?

Gideon: Well, it was like this. One of the soldiers had a strange dream. It was about a great big loaf of bread that rolled into the Midianite camp and completely flattened one of the tents. Then I knew that the soldier's dream was God's way of telling us that we would win.

Ripe: *(Strolling off with Rotten.)* Wow!

Rotten: Hey, I had a really funny dream. I had this dream that I was doing keep fit – you know, press-ups and all that stuff – not like me at all. It was really strange. Yes... and... *(They exit.)* (Gideon looks around, discovers he is alone, shrugs his shoulders and disappears back into the Time Shed. The Time Shed sound effects and lighting happen here.)*

* TALK TIME * TALK TIME * TALK TIME *

This story will need practice to get the timing right. You will also need an overhead projector acetate with the dashes drawn on, as below, for the game of Hangman at the end.

Let's see if we can remember what happened to Gideon. You can all help me by making different noises when I tell the story – OK? If I say 'Gideon', straight away you all say, 'Who, me?' and point to yourself, like this. *(Demonstrate.)* Let's practise that now. Ready? *(Practise saying 'Gideon', 'Who, me?', with the actions. You could make a placard for each word. Individual children could stand at the front and hold them up at the right moment.)* The other words go like this: 'Winepress' is 'Squelch, squelch' and you lift your feet up and down as if you are pressing grapes in a winepress. If I say 'frightened', you **bite your nails** like this. *(Demonstrate.)* For 'Angel', you say, 'Flap, flap' and you wave your arms up and down to flap your wings. When I say 'Midianites' you go 'Boo!', and cup your hands around your mouth, like this. Got it? Let's practise those. *(Practise.)* Now, I'll tell the story of Gideon quite slowly. You have to listen very carefully and make the right sounds and do the right actions for the right words. Here we go!

There was once a young man called **Gideon**. Yes. And **Gideon** – oh yes, he worked in a **winepress**. He wasn't very brave, in fact most of the time he was **frightened** because he was the smallest person in his family. One day while he was in the winepress he saw an **angel** who said to him, 'Hello, **Gideon**!'

'Yes, you', said the **angel**, 'I've got a job for you.'

'But I've already got one – in this **winepress**,' said **Gideon**, and he was now very **frightened**.

The **angel** said, 'Now listen **Gideon** – yes, you! I want you to go and fight the **Midianites**.'

'The... the... the... **Midianites**!' said **Gideon**.

'Yes – YOU!'

'But the reason I'm in this **winepress** is to get away from the **Midianites**. I mean the **Midianites** are big... and bad. And I'm **frightened**!'

'No need to be,' said the **angel**. 'God will help you, **Gideon** – yes, you!'

Eventually **Gideon** – yup – obeyed the **angel**, left the **winepress** and even though he was small and **frightened**, with just a few other men he defeated a whole army of **Midianites** because he trusted God and God helped him.

(If appropriate, repeat the story more quickly.)

I wonder what you think is the most important thing to remember about Gideon. Anyone got any ideas? Let's see if I agree with you. I've got a quick game of Hangman here *(switch on the overhead projector)* so when we have completed it, it will tell us something important we need to remember.

— — — — — —   — — — — — —   — — — .

— — —   — — — — — —   — — — — — —.

(Answer: Gideon trusted God. God helped Gideon.) If God helped Gideon, who else do you think he could help? *(Us.)* When might we need God to help us? *(If we are frightened or worried about something, when we are at school or when we want to do something we know we shouldn't, he can help us to be strong enough to say 'no'.)*

Let's pray now and ask God to help us, just as he helped Gideon when he felt very frightened.

Dear God, thank you that you know all about us and care for us. Thank you that you know when we feel weak, or worried, or frightened about something, like Gideon did. Please help us to trust you like Gideon did and to remember that if we ask you, you will help us when we need to be brave or do the right thing. Amen.

This story is taken from *Telling Tales* by Dave Hopwood, © 1993 and reproduced by kind permission. Copies are available from 40, Walton Road, Woking, Surrey, GU21 5DL.

Forfeits for Monkeying About

If you land on a square marked 'Forfeit', you can ask a Cabin Crew member or one of the Airport Staff in your Banana Bunch to do your forfeit for you. Choose any of these forfeits, but only one that has not already been done.

- Sing a nursery rhyme.
- Say the alphabet backwards.
- Get the Banana Bunch to sit in a circle and see how quickly you can hop around the outside.
- Shake the hand of everyone in your Banana Bunch.
- Whistle 'Oh, I Do Like To Be Beside the Seaside!'
- Say your ten times table.
- Bow or curtsey to five people in your Banana Bunch.
- Balance a book on your head for ten seconds.

MONKEYING ABOUT

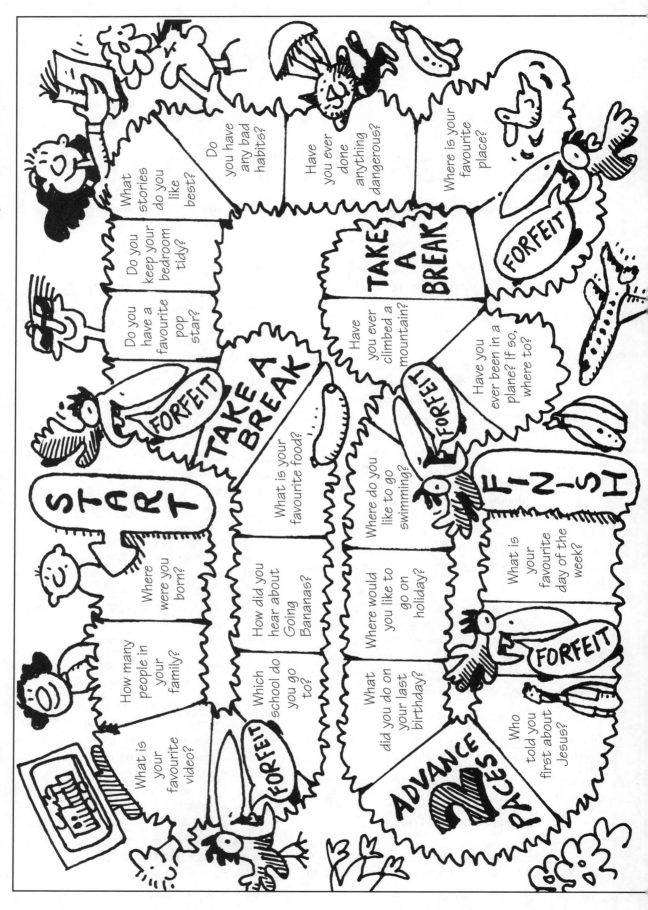

POSTCARD HOME

_____

_____

_____

_____

Dear

Today I went to GOING BANANAS!

Ripe was ☐ silly ☐ dead cool
☐ not sure what was going on.

I really enjoyed ☐ Bananaerobics
☐ Message in a bottle
☐ Singing about God.

I saw ☐ the Captain dancing
☐ the back of someone's head
☐ a banana flying by.

We learnt that Gideon went bananas and got rid of most of his army just when he needed to win a battle. The best thing I discovered about God was that.......................................
....
....

Lots of love from

Going Bananas

Discover some of the good news from the story of Gideon. Start at the top of the bread roll and write down every other letter on the dashes in the tent below. You'll need to go round the bread roll twice to get it all!

GIDEON

START HERE

TENT

DAY 3

Elijah

TEAM TIME

9.00

The team arrives.

After a short time to re-cap on yesterday, go straight into the Bible focus. Read Isaiah 42:1-4. Jesus was the perfect example of the Lord's Servant. Refer to the heading at the beginning of the chapter in the *Good News Bible*. Elijah was also a servant, and God wants us to be too. So what does that mean for us *today*, at **GOING BANANAS!**?

Look particularly at verse 1. God has *chosen* us, he *strengthens* us, especially when we are tired, halfway through the week, and he has *filled us with his Spirit*, so that he can work through us. We need to acknowledge our dependency on him.

Have a time of quiet, when everyone can respond to those verses in silent prayer, asking God to anoint them with his Spirit to be his servants and strengthen them for all that lies ahead in the next couple of hours. Then begin a short time of prayer for the day ahead, mentioning specific needs.

Go through the answers to the Big Questions for today.

BIG QUESTIONS

Bible passage
1 Kings 18:17-39

Who is God?
The only true God.

What is he like?
He's powerful, answers prayer, can do the 'impossible' and lets people know he exists.

Who 'went bananas' and why?
Elijah. Just when he wanted God to set fire to the altar he had built, he soaked it with water. He did it to show how great God was.

What did God do?
He revealed himself as the only true God and worthy of worship when he sent down fire at the contest on Mount Carmel.

What doesn't God want?
People to worship any god but him, disobedience to his commands.

What does he want?
People who worship and obey him wholeheartedly, people who risk everything for him.

9.15

Brief the team, explaining how to make Fierce Fiery Flames and Fabulous Flying Flags for Banana Bunches 1, and go through the rules for playing The Big Bucket Bonanza and Bananabrains and The Banana Piranha. Choose someone – perhaps one of the Banana Splits team – to operate the Banana Piranha puppet.

9.25

Everyone moves into position as usual – Elijah in the Time Shed, Passport Control, the Airport Staff, the Cabin Crew ready and the Banana Boys all set with the special effect for the hat trick.

Equipment needed

Banana Boys
* Copy of the day's programme
* Song words on overhead projector acetates
* Rotten's hat prepared with a length of cotton or fishing twine attached to it
* Quiz questions
* A large fruit basket
* The Banana Piranha
* Fishing net for catching Message in a Bottle (in the 'sea' at the back of the stage)
* Scissors
* An empty Message in a Bottle, and paper and pencils for new messages

Cabin Crew
* Name badges
* A bunch of exactly five bananas for each Banana Bunch
* Two pieces of card, one with 'True' printed on it, the other with 'False'

For Banana Bunches 1 each Banana Bunch will need:
* Several large sheets of paper with flame shapes drawn on them
* Lots of gold, yellow and orange paper and tissue paper
* Ready-mixed wallpaper paste or school glue in small pots with some brushes
* Sheets of A5 paper
* Non-bendy drinking straws, enough for one each
* Sticky tape * Felt-tip pens

For Banana Bunches 2 each Banana Bunch will need:
* Two buckets
* 12 plain disposable cups (either paper or plastic)

For Banana Bunches 3 each Banana Bunch will need:
* Blank speech bubble sheets
* Postcards Home (copied from the master on page 46)
* Felt-tip pens * Crayons
* Pencils

PROGRAMME AT A GLANCE

9.00
Team arrives for Bible focus and prayer

9.15
Team briefing

9.25
Into positions

Banana Bunches 1

Fun background music playing quietly

10.00
GOING BANANAS! song

10.05
Welcome/flight sequence/sound effects

10.10
Banana Boys 1

10.15
Songs 1 and 2

10.25
Bananabrains and The Banana Piranha

10.35
Song 3

10.40
Message in a Bottle

10.45
Video Story 3

10.50
The Time Shed Interview

11.00
Banana Splits

Fun background music playing quietly

11.15
Banana Bunches 2

11.25
Talk Time

11.35
Banana Bunches 3

11.55
Message in a Bottle

Return flight sequence/sound effects

11.58
GOING BANANAS! song

12.00
Disembarkation

12.15
Team de-briefing and prayer

PROGRAMME IN DETAIL

BIBLE PASSAGE 1 KINGS 18:17-39

KEY BIBLE VERSE PROVERBS 1:7

9.30

As usual, everyone should be in position, ready to welcome the Passengers, give them their badges and explain what they have to do for Banana Bunches 1.

BANANA BUNCHES 1:
MAKING GOING BANANAS! FIERCE FIERY FLAMES AND FABULOUS FLYING FLAGS

As the Passengers arrive, ask them which activity they would like to do. They can do both if they have time. Fierce Fiery Flames is a group activity and involves tearing the gold, yellow and orange paper into thin strips and pasting them onto the flame shapes. If they want to make a Fabulous Flying Flag, have the felt-tip pens ready, give them a sheet of A5 paper and explain that they can do any design they like. If the Cabin Crew make a flag as well, it will encourage the Passengers. When it is finished, attach it to a straw with sticky tape.

10.00

The Banana Band leads the **GOING BANANAS!** song.

10.05

The Captain welcomes everyone and leads into the flight sequence using the script on page 17, with lighting and sound effects from Bananas Wired for Sound and Light and a routine from an assistant. When the plane has landed, the Captain welcomes everyone to the island.

10.10

The Banana Boys enter with the dialogue based on Script 1 (page 43).

10.15

Ripe introduces the Passport Control team and leads two songs.

10.25

The Banana Boys explain Bananabrains and The Banana Piranha:

- Each Banana Bunch has a 'True' and 'False' card and a bunch of five bananas.
- When they have used their banana 'brains' as a group and decided on their answer, they display the appropriate card.
- If it is the correct answer, one passenger puts a banana into a basket on the stage. The basket should be placed *behind* Ripe and Rotten.
- The first team to get rid of all their bananas into the basket wins.

However, we have reckoned without The Banana Piranha – the vicious yellow sock puppet that grabs unsuspecting bananas! If he manages to grab a banana out of the basket, he can give it back to any Banana Bunch he chooses and they have to accept it. But if he is spotted by the Banana Boys, he has to stop and can't strike again until after the next question. The Banana Boys ask the children to warn them if they see The Banana Piranha, so that they can stop him. Of course, the idea is that this becomes a pantomime-style fiasco with the Banana Boys not spotting The Banana Piranha in time and all the children shouting, 'He's behind you!' The person who wears the puppet should pounce about three times during the questions, and any bananas The Banana Piranha manages to get should be re-distributed as fairly as possible.

TRUE OR FALSE QUESTIONS FOR BANANABRAINS AND THE BANANA PIRANHA:

Ripe and Rotten ask these from the front, first explaining the rules and also saying how later on we will be hearing about a competition that was held in Bible times to find out what was true and what was false. The whole Banana Bunch decide on the answer together and then display the appropriate card. If it is correct, one passenger puts a banana into the basket at the front.

1 On the fifth day of creation, God created the sun, moon and stars. True or false? (False – sea creatures and birds)

2 If all the bananas that are grown in the world in one year were placed end to end, they would stretch right around the world 1000 times. True or false? (False – more than 2000 times)

3 The boat Noah built was 450 feet or 140 metres long. True or false? (True)

4 Just when he needed to win a battle, Gideon went bananas and cut the size of his army from 32,000 men to only 300. True or false? (True)

5 Everybody we read about in the Bible followed the one true God. True or false? (False – some people worshipped idols made of wood and stone)

6 The Bible is not really just one book, but a whole library of sixty six different books which tell us all about God. True or false? (True)

7 This year is being celebrated as the 'Year of the Banana'. True or false? (False – it was 1995)

10.35

Rotten leads a song, but if Bananabrains has gone on longer than anticipated, it could be cut.

10.40

Ripe and Rotten discover the bottle and get a Passenger out to the front to fish it out of the 'sea' with the fishing net. The Banana Boys read some of the messages, and leave others for another day if necessary.

10.45

Story 3 of the **GOING BANANAS!** video.

10.50

THE TIME SHED INTERVIEW

Banana Boys interview Elijah.

11.00

Banana Splits are served to the children in their Banana Bunches. The Banana Boys announce the toilet break for Banana Bunches to go a bunch at a time, and the opportunity to write another message for Message in a Bottle. Any Passengers who want to could finish their Fantastic Flying Flags. During this time, Cabin Crew need to place their finished Fierce Fiery Flames on the stage, near where the Navigator will do the Talk Time.

11.15

BANANA BUNCHES 2: THE BIG BUCKET BONANZA

This game is wet! If you cannot play it outside and it is impossible to play indoors, then try the alternative activity suggestion.

The **Banana Boys** welcome everyone back and explain The Big Bucket Bonanza. Each Banana Bunch forms a

long line, as they did for the team game yesterday. Remembering what Elijah did with some jars of water, this is a chance for the Passengers and Crew to go bananas! Each Banana Bunch has two buckets, with one half-full of water. The person at the front of the line holds a disposable cup and, on the given signal, fills it from the bucket. The idea is to transfer the water to the second bucket which is placed opposite the line at the far end of the room, trying not to spill too much on the way. They run back and give the next person the cup. The game continues in relay fashion until the Banana Boys stop it.

The winners are the team with the most water in their second bucket. One of the Banana Splits team could act as judge and check it by pouring the water into a measuring jug to make quite sure it is fair!

Alternatively, each team could have twelve disposable cups, representing the stones Elijah used. Their task is to build an 'altar', in relay style. The first person in line takes a cup and runs to the opposite end of the room. When they return, the next person goes and gradually the 'altar' is built, pyramid-style. (It is best to put five cups at the base formed into a square, with one in the middle. Four cups go on top of them, followed by two and finally, one.) The winners are the team with most stones in their 'altar' after a set time.

11.25

Talk Time with the Navigator.

11.35

BANANA BUNCHES 3: BIG QUESTIONS

11.55

Someone from the Banana Band chooses a volunteer to throw today's new Message in a Bottle into the 'sea', followed by the return flight sequence with the Captain and appropriate sound effects.

11.58

The Captain suggests that all the Passengers wave their flags while singing the **GOING BANANAS!** song. The Captain reminds the Passengers to hand their badges in before leaving.

12.00

Disembarkation

12.15

Team de-briefing and prayer session

BANANA BOYS SCRIPT 1

For this sketch Rotten's hat needs to have a length of twine or thin cotton attached to it. The other end is held by a hidden team member – perhaps someone from Banana Splits. They yank the thread at the appropriate moment, so that the hat appears to blow away. It will need careful rehearsal.

(Ripe and Rotten enter. Ripe struggles with an armful of bananas and Rotten trails behind, yawning. Ripe puts the bananas down, and then notices the audience with a start.)

Ripe: Oh hello! I'd forgotten you would be here. The plane must have been early.

Rotten: *(Interrupts.)* Or we're late, more likely. It must be (time).

Ripe: And this is (place).

Rotten: And we're all **GOING BANANAS!**

*(Ripe and Rotten do the **GOING BANANAS!** shout.)*

Ripe: Right! Now we'd better get down to some work. *(Impatient.)* Come on, Rotten! We'll never get all the bananas picked on time.

Rotten: OK, OK. *(Yawns and staggers over to deck-chair. Sits down and puts hat over eyes.)*

Ripe: *(Counts bananas.)* One banana, two banana, three banana, four... *(Stops to build up to an enormous sneeze, which eventually happens in Rotten's direction. Rotten's hat is blown off by the force of the sneeze. Rotten stirs, finds his hat, puts it back on and goes back to sleep.)*

Ripe: *(Excitedly.)* That's it! If I blow Rotten's hat off and take it away, then he'll wake up and get to work. Yes! Here goes... (Takes a deep breath and blows hard. Nothing happens.)

Ripe: *(To audience.)* I know! If you lot all help me to blow really, really hard, it might work. Will you help me? *(Counts to three and has several attempts to blow the hat off. It finally works and Ripe removes hat.)*

Rotten: *(Wakes up.)* Hey! Where's my hat? *(Leaps out of chair and starts looking for it.)* I was wearing it. Where's it gone? That's strange... (Exits, looking for hat.)

Ripe: Rotten! Don't go away! There's work to be done! Rotten! Come back... *(Hurries out after Rotten.)*

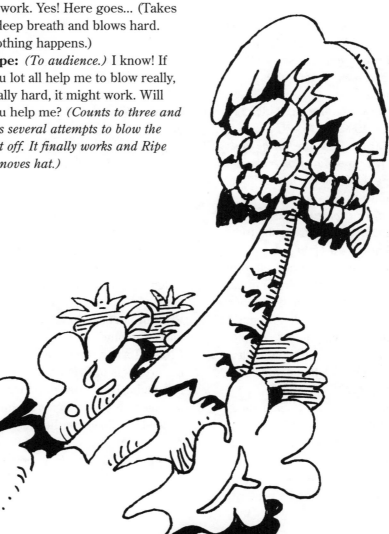

BANANA BOYS SCRIPT 2 WITH THE TIME SHED INTERVIEW

(Unnoticed by the Banana Boys, Elijah emerges from the Time Shed, brushing himself down.)

Rotten: Something's burning!

Ripe: You haven't left those banana fritters on, have you?

Rotten: No... No, it's more like... *(sniffing)*... the smell you get from the plug on your telly just before it bursts into flames.

Ripe: No, it's... *(sniffing)* a kind of... flame-grilled-burger smell, but burnt. *(Sniffing.)* Very burnt. *(By this time, they're on the floor sniffing Elijah's feet.)* It's *this*!

Rotten: I've never seen a flame-grilled burger wearing a sandal before.

Ripe: Oh, come on, Rotten. This is the 1990s!

Elijah: Excuse me. *(Ripe and Rotten jump out of their skins.)*

Ripe: Uh? What? Don't do that!

Elijah: Where am I?

Rotten: *(Pointing to where Elijah is standing.)* You're just... there!

Elijah: *(In a bit of a daze.)* Suddenly a ball of fire fell from the sky, the altar burst into flame, the bulls, the wood, the stones, the water, the earth all round the altar... everything was completely burnt up. Then in the middle of it all, I find myself in someone's... tool shed!

Rotten: *(Put out.)* *Time* Shed actually.

Ripe: *(To Elijah.)* Are you... are you...?

Rotten: *(Interrupting.)* A flame-grilled burger or a banana fritter?

Ripe: *(To Rotten.)* Keep quiet!... *(To Elijah.)* Elijah?

Elijah: *(Coming out of his daze.)* Eh? What?... Oh... yes. How do you do?

Rotten: We're fine, but you smell!

Ripe: *(To Rotten.)* Sssshh!

Rotten: A *lot*!

Elijah: *(Ignoring Rotten.)* You must be Ripe and Rotten. I *know* these things. And this must be... (name of place)... (date) and

GOING BANANAS!

Ripe: If you happy or you're sad...

Rotten: If you're gloomy or you're glad...

All: Let's all go bananas!

Rotten: Why do you smell so much?

Elijah: Well, there was a big fire.

Rotten: Shall I call the fire brigade?

Elijah: *(Shaking his head.)* Let me explain. I wanted the people of Israel to know that our Lord is the true God, not that stone thing they bow down and worship called Baal. God of the weather? Huh!

Rotten: Sounds more like a garden gnome!

Elijah: Exactly. So I challenged the prophets of Baal on the mountain. They prayed to their so-called god to try and get him to send fire down on the altar, and he didn't.

Ripe: Well, he *wouldn't*... being stone... *would* he?

Elijah: But the God of Israel *did*. Crash! Woomph! All the prophets of Baal screamed, 'The Lord is God! The Lord is God!' I *think* they got the message! And that's why I smell like a... *what* did you call it?... flame-grilled burger? *(Turning to go back into the Time Shed.)*

Ripe: *(Picking up a* Good News Bible *and flicking it open to the right page.)* Hey! There's a bit about you in this book!

Elijah: *(Peering over Ripe's shoulder.)* What book is that then?

Ripe: It's the Bible. Most of it hadn't been written when you were around, but this bit says... *(Reads 1 Kings 18:36-39 from the Good News Bible.)*

Elijah: Well, that's exactly what happened! But, I'm afraid I must be going – I've got work to do. *(Disappearing inside the Time Shed.)*

Rotten: *(Calling after him.)* You haven't got a dog, have you? The bloke we had here two days ago had a dog. I don't like dogs... *(Exit. Time Shed Routine.)*

* TALK TIME * TALK TIME * TALK TIME *

For this talk you will need twelve large stones. You may be able to borrow them from a garden rockery, or collect them from a beach. Otherwise, you could persuade a local garden centre to lend you some! You will also need the Fierce Fiery Flames which were placed at the side of the stage earlier, but leave them there until you come to the appropriate point in the talk. Have a bucket ready with a small amount of water in it, with a cloth to mop it up afterwards!

Is it me, or is it cold in here? I guess you lot aren't cold but I could do with warming my hands by a nice fire. *(Laughing.)* I suppose that's what Elijah did really, although *he* didn't need any matches! What he did need though were twelve large stones like these. *(Get the stones and carry on talking while you start to build them into an altar.)* Can you remember what he did with them? Yes! Just like this, he built them into an altar – an altar ready for some meat to be sacrificed to God as a burnt offering. To us it sounds a strange thing to do, but in Bible times it was a special way of showing God how great he was.

Elijah knew that, and he knew that God was the one true God, but the king and the priests who worshipped Baal didn't. Well, not to start with anyway. *They* prayed to an idol made out of a lump of stone! So it was hardly surprising that he didn't answer them. *(Pick up the bucket and pretend to pour water on the altar you have built.)* And then Elijah went bananas! *(To Passengers, as you pour the water.)* Sorry! Did I splash you? Don't get wet! But *more* importantly, careful you don't get burnt! Keep back! *(As you say this, pick up the flames made earlier and drop them on top of the altar.)* Mind out! *Now* who was the only true God? That meant Baal was false. Who can remember what happened next? The Bible tells us. *(Read 1 Kings 18:39.)*

Well, I've got a fire to warm my hands on now. Next time you see a fire, think about this story and how great and powerful and true God is.

* TALK TIME * TALK TIME * TALK TIME *

POSTCARD HOME

(stamp: Going Bananas)

Dear

Today I went to GOING BANANAS!

Our Cabin Crew were ☐ amazing
☐ totally worn out
☐ dressed in super cool gear.

We kept
☐ playing excellent games
☐ quiet ☐ tropical fish.

I had ☐ a brainwave ☐ a scrummy biscuit
☐ stomache ache.

We learnt that Elijah went bananas and soaked the altar he wanted God to burn up. The best thing I discovered about God was that

....

....

....

Lots of love from

ELIJAH

Find all the words below in the word square. They go across or down only. Cross out each letter you use.

MOUNT   CARMEL   WORSHIP
PROPHETS   LORD   FIRE
PRAYED   WATER   TRUE
OBEY   ISRAEL

M	W	C	A	R	M	E	L	L
O	O	T	F	H	E	L	L	O
U	R	O	I	W	R	D	R	R
N	S	P	R	A	Y	E	D	D
T	H	I	E	T	R	U	E	E
S	I	O	B	E	Y	G	O	O
D	P	I	S	R	A	E	L	L
P	R	O	P	H	E	T	S	S

Now start at the top of the square. Read from left to right and write on the dashes all the letters you haven't crossed out. Put one letter on each dash, in the order you come to them.

Now read the secret message!

— !

DAY 4 Zacchaeus

TEAM TIME

9.00

The team assembles, wearing t-shirts and name badges as usual. Re-cap briefly on yesterday before the Bible focus.

Divide the team into several small groups and ask them to look at the Parable of the Lost Sheep (Matthew 18:10-14). Prompted particularly by verses 10 and 14, encourage them to focus on the particular needs of children in their Banana Bunch. Give each Banana Bunch a list of the children in their group. Ask each small group to pray for every child on their list *by name*, mentioning specific needs, encouragements or problems if appropriate.

Go through the answers to the Big Questions that everyone will discuss in Banana Bunches today.

BIG QUESTIONS

Bible passage
Luke 19:1-10

Who is God?
The Saviour.

What is he like?
He cares for individuals, searches for 'lost' people, wants to save them and has a sense of mission for them ('I must stay in your house today').

Who 'went bananas' and why?
Zacchaeus, a grown man and a social outcast climbed a tree because he wanted to see Jesus. Then he gave all his money away.

What did God do?
He found Zacchaeus and saved him.

What doesn't God want?
People to think that others don't count in God's sight.

What does he want?
People who are willing to 'go bananas' for him, joy in people's lives, and action which shows that faith is real.

9.15

Brief the team and go through the day's programme. Demonstrate how to make a tree for The Terrific Tropical Tree Trunk Test. If time allows, do a very quick dummy-run of the Bananadrama for Banana Bunches 2. Tell the team about Banana Skins.

9.25

Passport Control, the Cabin Crew and the Banana Band all need to be ready and in position. Zacchaeus should be concealed in the Time Shed – his big entrance will be on his knees, so that he can give the impression of being very short. The Captain and Banana Boys are ready for their entrance and Bananas Wired for Sound and Light for their cue.

Equipment needed

Banana Boys
* Copy of the day's programme
* Song words on overhead projector acetates
* A custard pie on a paper plate (perfume-free shaving foam works well)
* Whistle
* Workout tape for Bananaerobics
* Message in a Bottle with paper and pencils
* A fishing net * Scissors

Cabin Crew
* Name badges (plus some spares for new arrivals)

For Banana Bunches 1 each Banana Bunch will need:
* Roll of brown wrapping paper
* Large sheets of green paper

* Small sheets of yellow paper
* Reel of sticky tape
* Scissors * Pencils

For Banana Bunches 2 each Banana Bunch will need:
* A Good News Bible
* The tree you made earlier
* Some plain tea towels and string to make head coverings for actors (optional)
* A chair

For Banana Bunches 3 each Banana Bunch will need:
* Blank speech bubble sheets
* Postcards Home from the master on page 53, enough for one each, plus a few spares
* Felt-tip pens * Crayons
* Scissors

PROGRAMME AT A GLANCE

9.00
Team arrives for Bible focus and prayer

9.15
Team briefing

9.25
Into positions

Banana Bunches 1

Fun background music playing quietly

10.00
GOING BANANAS! song

10.03
Welcome/flight sequence/sound effects

10.10
Banana Boys 1

10.35
Song 1

10.40
Video Story 4

10.50
Banana Splits

Fun background music playing quietly

11.00
Whistle for Banana Skins

11.05
The Time Shed Interview

11.12
Song 2

Prayers

11.20
Banana Bunches 2

11.30
Bananaerobics, to be omitted if the programme is running late

11.35
Talk Time

11.40
Banana Bunches 3

11.50
Prayer

11.55
Throw Message in a Bottle into the 'sea'

Return flight sequence/sound effects

11.58
GOING BANANAS! song

12.00
Disembarkation

12.15
Team de-briefing and prayer

PROGRAMME IN DETAIL

BIBLE PASSAGE LUKE 19:1-10

KEY BIBLE VERSE MATTHEW 18:3

9.30

BANANA BUNCHES 1:
THE TERRIFIC TROPICAL TREE TRUNK TEST

The Passengers join in with this activity as they arrive. Explain that today's story will have a tree in it. The tree could represent the one that Zacchaeus climbed. It might also double up as a banana tree which could then be used to decorate the venue and/or the church for the finale on Sunday. Each Banana Bunch can make their tree in whatever way they like, but as a guideline, pull the roll of brown paper out from the centre of the roll to form the trunk. The children can cut out green palm leaves and paste them on, with bananas made from the yellow paper. The Banana Band plays in the background while this is going on.

9.55

The Cabin Crew clear up the scraps of paper and help the children to add the finishing touches to the tree, ready for inspection by the Banana Boys later.

10.00

The Banana Band lead the **GOING BANANAS!** song with everyone joining in.

10.03

The Captain welcomes Passengers on board and explains the location of the fire exits, the use of toilets (only at Banana Splits time unless it is an absolute emergency!) and the rules about keeping away from the stage area because of the electrical equipment. He goes through the take-off procedure as usual, with lights and sound effects from Bananas Wired for Sound and Light.

10.08

The Captain welcomes the Passengers to the island and tells them to watch out for the Banana Boys.

10.10

The Banana Boys use Script 1 from page 50.

10.15

Ripe introduces the Banana Splits team and leads everyone in a suitable show of appreciation. Rotten warns of Banana Skins to come, identified by a whistle. Banana Skins, which could be inserted into the programme more than once if necessary, means standing up, doing five star jumps and then sitting down again. Ripe and Rotten demonstrate and then get everyone to practise, making sure they are aware of the people near them so that it is safe!

10.25

Ripe discovers another Message in a Bottle. He chooses a volunteer from the audience. Perhaps the team could decide beforehand who this should be – maybe someone with a birthday or a special need. They come out to the front and use the fishing net to retrieve the bottle. Ripe opens it and reads out the messages, with the exception of the prayers, which will be read later.

10.35

Rotten introduces and leads a song.

10.40

Story 4 of the **GOING BANANAS!** video.

10.50

Banana Splits are served to the Banana Bunches. Everyone stays sitting in their Banana Bunches and the trays are taken to them. Cabin Crew members remind the children that everyone goes to the toilet one Banana Bunch at a time so they will have to wait their turn. While they are waiting they could write a message and put it in the bottle. The Cabin Crew could also take the opportunity to chat about the video they have just seen.

11.00

Ripe welcomes everyone back and makes the sound for Banana Skins.

11.05

THE TIME SHED INTERVIEW

Banana Boys interview Zacchaeus.

(The Banana Boys use Script 2 on page 51 at this point.)

11.10

The Time Shed procedure is reversed as usual.

11.12

Ripe and Rotten introduce and lead a song, followed by any prayers from Message in A Bottle, or simple prayers read from a book. Some prayer resources are suggested on page 62.

11.20

BANANA BUNCHES 2:
BANANADRAMA IN BANANA BUNCHES

Ripe and Rotten explain how each group has ten minutes to act out the story of Zacchaeus for themselves. The Cabin Crew can use the Bible verses as a narrative. The tree made earlier could be propped against a chair so that Zacchaeus can 'climb' it. While this is happening, Ripe and Rotten circulate, making encouraging comments about the trees and the drama.

11.30

Ripe and Rotten lead a gentle aerobics routine to music for Bananaerobics.

11.35

The Navigator does the Talk Time using the outline on page 52.

11.40

BANANA BUNCHES 3: BIG QUESTIONS

11.50

The Navigator gets everyone together again and leads a simple prayer, thanking God that he sent Jesus to be our friend, just as he was Zacchaeus' friend.

11.55

A Passenger is chosen to throw the Message in a Bottle into the 'sea' and then the Captain talks everyone through the return flight, with sound effects and lighting from Bananas Wired for Sound and Light. The Captain reminds everyone that there is another GOING BANANAS! tomorrow and also a special GOING BANANAS! in church on Sunday.

11.58

The Banana Band lead the GOING BANANAS! song.

12.00

The Captain leads the disembarkation procedure, with the Passengers leaving one Banana Bunch at a time.

12.15

The team stay for a de-brief and time of prayer.

BANANA BOYS SCRIPT 1

The Banana Boys need a custard pie on a paper plate, placed out of sight

Ripe: Hello again!

Rotten: *(Nudges Ripe and points to himself.)* No, you dope, my name's not again, it's Rotten.

Ripe: *(Laughs.)* I know, I wouldn't like a name like that either! Anyway, I was just saying hello to all these these Passengers and Cabin Crew. I wonder if they can say hello back?

Rotten: *(Interrupts.)* I can! Hello, back.

Ripe: *(Ignores Rotten and speaks to audience.)* Can you all say hello to us after three? One, two, three...

*(Rotten and Ripe do the **GOING BANANAS!** shout)*

Rotten: All that noise has made me feel quite tired. I think I'll just sit down for a bit. *(Walks towards deck-chair, but is stopped by Ripe.)*

Ripe: Oh no you won't.

Rotten: Oh yes I will!

(Pantomime style banter follows, involving the audience, during which time Rotten sneaks into his chair, puts his hat on over his eyes and starts to snore loudly.)

Ripe: *(Notices Rotten asleep.)* Oh no! Now look what he's gone and done. Now we'll never get any bananas picked. Wait a minute... I've got an idea! I was just making some banana custard. What if I get Rotten to help me? He likes his food, so he won't be able to resist it. *(Calls to Rotten.)* Tea time! *(No response at all from Rotten, who continues to snore loudly.)* Hey you! Wake up! *(Shakes him, with no response.)* What am I going to do now? *(To audience.)* Will you lot help me wake him up? *(Gets audience to shout 'Wake up, Rotten' after a count of three. After a couple of attempts, Rotten wakes up.)*

Rotten: Uh? What?

Ripe: It's tea time. I need you to help me with the banana custard.

Rotten: Yum yum! My favourite! *(Rubs his eyes, yawns and staggers sleepily towards Ripe who is busy getting a custard pie.)*

Ripe: *(Holds the custard pie triumphantly and turns around innocently at just the right moment so that it lands in Rottens face.)* What did you say?

Rotten: *(Removes custard pie and wipes his face.)* I *said* it was my favourite!

Ripe: *(To audience.)* That's just as well, isn't it? *(Laughs.)*

Rotten: Talking of food, it's time to meet the Banana Splits!

BANANA BOYS SCRIPT 2 WITH THE TIME SHED INTERVIEW

This begins with the same routine for the Time Shed as on Day 1, starting with Ripe and Rotten doing the countdown, followed by the sound and lighting effects. Before Ripe has the chance to go to the door of the Time Shed, Zacchaeus bursts out with a bag of coins.

Zac: *(Ignoring Ripe and Rotten and addressing the children and team members.)* 'Ere, have I ever ripped you off? You know, taken more money off you than I should?... 'Ow much?... That's not enough! I'll give you four times that much!... Anyone else? *(To Ripe.)* Oh yeah, I remember *you*. Wife, ten children, six goats and I took just about every penny you had in taxes. Err... sorry about that. Look, I'll make it up to you.

Ripe: I think you've got me mixed up with someone else. I don't know who you are or...

Zac: What? Everyone in Jericho knows Zac the tax man! *(Suddenly noticing where he is.)* Err, wait a minute. This *isn't* Jericho, is it?

Rotten: *(Aside.)* Cor, he's bright!

Ripe: No, this is... (name of place), it's... (date), we're the Banana Boys and this is **GOING BANANAS!**

Rotten: If you're happy or you're sad...

Ripe: If you're gloomy or you're glad...

All: Let's all go bananas!

Rotten: *(Realizing who Zac is.)* Hang on, *now* I remember. You're that Zacchaeus bloke, from Jesus' time – that tiny tax man everyone hated!

Ripe: *(Pulling a face and making to run off in horror.)* Excuse me, I'll be back with you shortly.

Rotten: *(Pulling Ripe back.)* Don't call him Shortly! It's rude!

Zac: Well, everyone *used* to hate me, but a couple of people actually smiled at me today, when I gave them their money back.

Ripe: *(To Zac.)* But why are you giving money *back* to people? Have you gone bananas or what?

Zac: Maybe. People thought I was mad when I shinned up that tree to see Jesus, so I expect they'll say the same about me giving people's money back.

Ripe: But how come you've changed?

Zac: Jesus came to my house... to *my* house.

Rotten: And?

Zac: And he wanted to be my friend.

Rotten: What, you? Titch? Zac the rip-off man? The one everyone loved to hate? Friend of the filthy, slimy, greasy Romans?

Ripe: Ssshh!

Zac: *(To Rotten.)* Yeah, amazing, isn't it? I was totally gobsmacked myself. There were loads of people around who were much nicer, taller and more important than me. But when Jesus came to my house, I knew that he knew how mean and horrible I was... and he still cared!

Ripe: But you haven't answered my question about why you're giving all this money away.

Rotten: Yeah, you haven't answered his question! Go on, answer his question!

Zac: Well, having a friend is brilliant. But having Jesus as a friend is worth more than all the money in the world! And now I've met him, I want to give, not take... I reckon he'd give you everything he had if you needed it... Still, I can't hang around here all day talking to you. I've got money to give away!

(Zac bustles into the Time Shed. Routine.)

* TALK TIME * TALK TIME * TALK TIME *

(For this Talk Time you will need two simple placards made from sheets of card, one with the word 'Before' and the other with the word 'After' printed on it. Each needs to be attached to a stick, such as a garden cane. Keep them out of sight, but hold the appropriate one up briefly each time you mention either word.)

He was a cheat – nobody liked him. So… he was probably lonely and unhappy. That was **before**. *(Show the placard with the word 'Before' on it.)*

Before what? Before he went bananas – for the first time – and climbed a tree. It made sense *really* because he couldn't see a thing, but everyone else must have laughed and thought he'd gone bananas.

And then he went completely bananas! He'd spent all his time getting as much money as he could out of people and then suddenly – **after** *(Show 'After' placard.)* – he gave it all back. Bananas!

After what? What happened? What, or who, made the difference?

It was Jesus of course. Jesus, God's son. **Before** he met Jesus and got things sorted out, Zacchaeus was doing things God *didn't* want. But **after** he became Jesus' friend he changed and he began to do things God *did* want. *(If they are on display, indicate the speech bubbles the Banana Bunches have completed so far.)*

What about you? Perhaps, a bit like Zacchaeus, you think Jesus isn't interested in you. Well, he is! Just as he was interested in Zacchaeus. And as we've found out, having Jesus as his friend made a big difference to Zacchaeus.

Perhaps **before GOING BANANAS!** you hadn't thought about God very much. Maybe now you are starting to think about the things God doesn't want in your life and how you can do the things God does want. Perhaps, like Zacchaeus, you will change as you get to know Jesus as your friend.

If you want to know more about how you can do that, have a chat with your Cabin Crew member afterwards.

And what will you do **after GOING BANANAS!**, to help you carry on doing what God wants? (Here you could mention your Sunday activities or any follow-up events or clubs to which the children could come along.) It might not always be easy. You may get laughed at. Perhaps your friends will think you have gone bananas.

Remember Noah whom we met earlier this week? Everyone probably laughed at him and said he had gone bananas because he did what God wanted. It made sense in the end, didn't it? And if you know, like Elijah did, how mighty and powerful God is, you don't need to worry! You can remember that just as he was with Gideon and helped him, God is with you too and can help you, even when you feel frightened.

* TALK TIME * TALK TIME * TALK TIME *

POSTCARD HOME

Lots of love from

....

....

.... that was God about discovered
I thing best The Jesus. see to tree a climbed
and bananas went Zacchaeus that learnt We

□ sleep   □ keep talking to God
□ watch out for the Banana Piranha   I must
□ not amused by Rotten's jokes.
□ very well behaved
□ airsick in the plane   I was
□ tricks on everyone.
□ brilliantly   □ tiddlywinks   The Banana Band played

Today I went to GOING BANANAS!
Dear

Going Bananas

ZACCHAEUS

❀ = a   ✳ = d   ❋ = e   ✧ = G   ✴ = h   ✺ = i   ★ = J
● = l   ○ = m   ■ = n   ▢ = o   ▭ = p   ✪ = r   ▲ = s
▼ = t   ◆ = u   ❖ = v   ◗ = w   ▮ = y

DAY 5 Jemima

the woman with the jar of perfume

TEAM TIME

9.00

The team arrives.

Have a brief re-cap on yesterday and an update on plans for the Sunday all-age worship, as well as any specific plans for follow-up. Mention the Talk Time, which will give a low-key opportunity for Passengers to respond to the Gospel message. The emphasis will be on becoming a friend of God – encourage the Cabin Crew to use that illustration. Hand out copies of *The Good News* (see page 62) and go through it with the team, step by step, so that everyone is familiar with the content.

Move into the Bible focus and read Ephesians 5:1-2 together. These verses reinforce the main teaching point from today's story and are a reminder of how we should behave. We are told to be controlled by love, Christ-like and pleasing to God. Invite the team to brainstorm for a couple of minutes in twos and threes on practical ways in which we can demonstrate these qualities to the Passengers. Finish with a time of prayer.

Go through the answers to the Big Questions for today.

BIG QUESTIONS

Bible passage
Luke 7:36-50

Who is God?
Jesus

What is he like?
He wants to be close to people who have gone wrong, enjoys their company and loving response, he loves them enough to die for them.

Who 'went bananas' and why?
The woman with the jar of perfume. She poured lots of expensive perfume over Jesus' feet, because she was really sorry for all the wrong things she had done. She wanted to show Jesus that she loved him.

What did God do?
He accepted and applauded her loving gesture, and defended the 'wastefulness' of her action.

What doesn't God want?
Apathy towards him, a distance between himself and sinful people, criticism of those who 'go bananas' out of love for him.

What does he want?
His followers to show how much they love him, love and action that 'extravagance' in response to him, costs, humility, loyalty, understanding, devotion.

9.15

Brief the team, explaining how to make Clever Costumes for Banana Bunches 1. Explain the Guess the Smell game for Banana Bunches 2.

9.25

The team take up their positions as usual, with Jemima concealed in the Time Shed.

Equipment needed

Banana Boys
* Copy of the day's programme
* Song words on overhead projector acetates
* 15 cups with smelly substances for Banana Bunches 2
* Whistle for Banana Skins
* Workout Tape for Bananaerobics
* Banana Bin, banana-shaped paper and pencils
* A blindfold, a dozen eggs and a small packet of cornflakes

Cabin Crew
* Name badges

For Banana Bunches 1 each Banana Bunch will need:
* Raw materials for Clever Costumes, as detailed in description on page 55
* Sticky tape * Staplers
* Glue * Spreaders
* Scissors * Cotton wool
* Elastic * Face paints

For Banana Bunches 2 each Banana Bunch will need:
* Paper and a pencil for Guess the Smell

For Banana Bunches 3 each Banana Bunch will need:
* Blank speech bubble sheets
* Postcards Home (copied from the master on page 60)
* Felt-tip pens * Crayons
* Pencils

PROGRAMME AT A GLANCE

9.00 Team arrives for Bible focus and prayer

9.15 Team briefing

9.25 Into positions
Banana Bunches 1
Fun background music playing quietly

10.00 GOING BANANAS! song

10.05 Welcome/flight sequence/sound effects

10.10 Banana Boys welcome/introductions and explanation of Banana Skins

10.15 Parade of Clever Costumes

10.20 Song 1

10.25 Banana Boys 1

10.30 Bananaerobics

10.35 Video Story 5

10.45 Banana Splits

10.55 Whistle for Banana Skins

11.05 Song 2

11.10 Mashed Bananas

11.15 Banana Bunches 2

11.25 The Time Shed Interview

11.30 Talk Time

11.35 Banana Bunches 3
Prayer in groups

11.55 Return flight sequence/sound effects

11.58 GOING BANANAS! song

12.00 Disembarkation

12.15 Team de-briefing and prayer

PROGRAMME IN DETAIL

BIBLE PASSAGE LUKE 7:36-50

KEY BIBLE VERSES PROVERBS 3:5,6

9.30

Everyone should be in position, with Passport Control ready to hand out publicity for the Sunday all-age worship, if appropriate. Jemima should be concealed in the Time Shed. Cabin Crew should be well prepared, with all the materials ready for the Passengers to get going with Creating Cever Costumes.

BANANA BUNCHES 1:
CREATING CLEVER COSTUMES

These are in the context of a end-of-the-week celebration and they also link in with today's story, which is about a 'dinner party' at Simon's home where the guests would have been in their best clothes. The Passengers can make their own Clever Costumes from different coloured bin liners, with holes cut out for the arms and neck. They can attach decorations made from tissue or crêpe paper, using a stapler, sticky tape or glue. Cloaks can also be created from bin liners, and strips of paper or plastic tied, pleated or folded in a bow make good sashes or belts. Boys could make waistcoats and bow-ties, or they may prefer to create their own biblical-style outfits from a selection of old clothes, sheets, plain tea towels, belts and string. Beards can be made from cotton wool and elastic, or with face paints.

It may sound daunting, but this is the sort of activity which the Passengers will get into very quickly. Cabin Crew will need to watch out for any who are struggling and give them a hand. Encourage the Passengers to take it in turns to help each other create their Clever Costumes. Bear in mind that they need to make the outfits on themselves, wear them for the rest of the session and then go home in them! A very useful book which is full of ideas, is *The Dressing-Up Book* by Wendy Baker, published by Two-Can. It can be ordered from bookshops and is well worth obtaining.

10.00

The Banana Band leads the **GOING BANANAS!** song.

10.05

The Captain welcomes the Passengers, and after the usual notices mentions the special flight to Banana Island on Sunday, giving a few details to whet the Passengers' appetites. He leads into the flight sequence, adapting the script on page 17.

Sound effects and lighting as usual.

10.10

The Banana Boys say hello to the children. They introduce Bananas Wired for Sound and Light and Yes! We Have Some Bananas!. They explain Banana Skins, which happens when the horn is blown. Each Banana Bunch has to take off their shoes and arrange them on the floor into the letters GB (for **GOING BANANAS!**). All the shoes must be used, and when the task is completed the Banana Bunch must sit down in a circle around their letters.

10.15

Ripe and Rotten explain that today is a bit like a party as it has been such a good week at **GOING BANANAS!** Also, they mention that later on the Bible story takes place at a grand dinner party, which is why everyone is dressing up. They announce a special parade of all the Clever Costumes, with all the Passengers walking around in a large circle. All the team are suitably appreciative and The Banana Boys congratulate the Passengers.

10.20

Ripe introduces and leads a song. Rotten stays out of sight, ready for the sketch.

10.25

The Banana Boys use Script 1 from page 57.

10.30

Bananaerobics.

10.35

Story 5 of the **GOING BANANAS!** video.

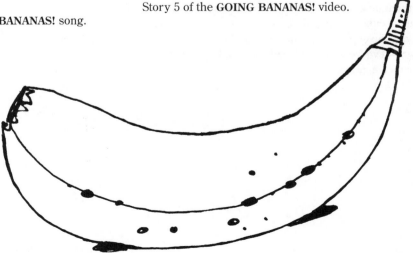

10.45

Time for Banana Splits, with special party food. The Banana Splits team wear funny hats and the trays are decorated with streamers. The Banana Boys announce that anyone who wants to sign up for Mashed Bananas must put their piece of paper in the Banana Bin by the end of Banana Splits. The Banana Band plays fun, background music.

10.55

The Banana Boys blow the horn for Banana Skins and then circulate, judging each Banana Bunch.

11.05

Rotten introduces and leads song 2.

11.10

The Banana Boys announce Mashed Bananas, which is a game called 'Rip yer socks off!'. Ripe and Rotten pick four names out of the Banana Bin. The four contestants take off their shoes and stand on the stage. They have to get their socks off as quickly as they can, but they are not allowed to use their hands, which they must keep behind their backs. The winner is the first person to get both their socks off. Someone from Passport Control acts as judge. It can be organised as a heat if there is time.

11.15

THE BANANA BOYS INTRODUCE AND ORGANISE BANANA BUNCHES 2: GUESS THE SMELL

You will need fifteen disposable cups, with the following substances in them: mint sauce, blackcurrant juice, salad cream, mustard, vinegar, coffee, tea, onion, yeast extract (Marmite or Vegemite), peanut butter, drinking chocolate, peppermint, soap powder, shampoo and disinfectant. Each cup will need to be covered with paper. Punch a few holes in each cover and attach with an elastic band. Number the cups clearly with a spirit marker and divide them between the Banana Bunches. Give each group a minute to identify their smells and write them on a piece of paper. On a given signal, the batches of cups are passed on to another Banana Bunch. That way, the cups circulate around all the groups. At the end, when everyone has finished, Banana Boys read out the correct answers.

11.25

When Guess the Smell has finished, the lighting and sound effects start for The Time Shed Interview, using the script on page 58.

11.30

Talk Time with the Navigator, using the script on page 59.

11.35

BANANA BUNCHES 3: BIG QUESTIONS

The Passengers go into their Banana Bunches for the last time. They complete the speech bubbles and the Postcards Home, copied from the master on page 60. Just before they are due to finish, the Navigator sets up a brief time of prayer in the Banana Bunches. A Bible is passed around the circle and whoever is holding it can either pray out loud, or quietly. When they've finished, they pass the Bible on to the next person.

11.55

The Captain announces the special event in church and details of any follow-up activities, and then leads into the return flight procedure as usual.

11.58

The Banana Band plays the **GOING BANANAS!** song.

12.00

The Captain announces Disembarkation and dismisses the Passengers a Banana Bunch at a time.

12.15

The team meet to de-brief, pray and collapse in a heap!

BANANA BOYS SCRIPT 1

For this sketch, which includes a messy party game, you will need a blindfold, a dozen eggs and a small packet of cornflakes. If the trick is inappropriate for any reason, substitute something similar.
(Ripe enters, looking around furtively.)

Ripe: Hey, you lot! Has anyone seen Rotten? No? Oh good! I want you all to help me play a trick on him and I need to explain it before he arrives. Can you listen up? This is what's going to happen. I'm going to put these eggs all over the ground and when Rotten has seen where they are, I shall blindfold him and tell him to walk across here *(indicates stage area)* without treading on any eggs. But, what he won't know is that just before he starts, I shall take away the eggs and spread these cornflakes on the ground instead. Now, you lot have to pretend that the eggs are still there and then when he treads on the cornflakes and they make a noise, he'll think he's broken an egg. If you can all groan loudly and make ugh noises when he thinks he's trodden on one, it will add to the fun. Everybody got that? Remember, don't give the secret away. Shhh! Here he comes...

When Rotten enters, Ripe explains that he has arranged a special test of skill to qualify him for an Advanced Diploma in Banana Picking. He sets the 'test' up, putting the eggs out and then blindfolding Rotten. To conceal the noise of cornflakes being substituted for eggs, Ripe could do the **GOING BANANAS!** *shout.*
Rotten: *(After the trick.)* Well! And I thought I was going to get extra qualifications as a banana picker!
Ripe: Tell you what, you could get some some exercise instead. That way, at least you will be fit for the job! *(Ripe now introduces Bananaerobics.)*

BANANA BOYS SCRIPT 2 WITH THE TIME SHED INTERVIEW

Time Shed routine as usual. After the sound effects stop, Ripe and Rotten sniff around, coming towards the Time Shed door backwards. They bump into Jemima as she also comes out of the Time Shed backwards, looking around warily.

Ripe: *(Sniffs.)* What's that funny smell, Rotten?

Rotten: I don't think it's anything *rotten*. It smells too nice for that.

Ripe: *(Exasperated.)* No! *(Sniffs.)* It's definitely not a flame-grilled burger. It's... kind of sweet. You wearing aftershave, Rotten?

Rotten: Don't be daft! No point shaving on Banana Island. *(Sniffs.)* No, it's more of a... *(Jemima, Ripe and Rotten all bump into each other backwards. All jump.)*

Ripe: Ooops! Sorry, didn't see you there!

Jemima: *(Clearly upset, but very relieved.)* Oh, I thought you were Simon and the others. They were saying horrible things about me and they were angry, then... suddenly... I found myself inside this... er... tool shed.

Rotten: *Time* Shed, actually.

Ripe: No, we're not Simon and the others. We're the Banana Boys, Ripe and Rotten. We live here on Banana Island and this is **GOING BANANAS!** *(Ripe and Rotten do the **GOING BANANAS!** shout.)*

Jemima: Well, my name's Jemima, but you probably won't want to know me. I've done lots of bad things. The only person who cares about me is Jesus and he's forgiven me for all those wrong things in my life.

Rotten: Sounds like Jesus to me!

Jemima: That's right. I wanted to show him that I was *really* sorry and to sort of... well... say *thank you*.

Ripe: So how did you do that?

Jemima: To start with, I couldn't help crying over Jesus, because I felt so ashamed and sorry for the things I've done. His feet got really wet.

Rotten: Did you say his feet? Don't you mean his shoulder? That's the usual place to cry on.

Jemima: He was lying at the table, having a meal. I was kneeling at his feet.

Rotten: Oh, I see...

Jemima: First of all I had to dry his feet, so I used my long hair. Then I poured some perfume on them.

Rotten: Did you say perfume? On Jesus' *feet?*

Jemima: Yes. it was to make them fresh and cool. It's been such a hot, dusty day.

Ripe: Sounds good to me! My feet are hot and sticky.

Rotten: I bet they're smelly too!

Ripe: They wouldn't be with some perfume on them. *(To Jemima.)* Couldn't you have used something a bit cheaper than perfume? It's very expensive.

Rotten: Well, I expect you only used a teeny tiny bit, didn't you?

Jemima: Oh no! I used the whole jar and it was very expensive. It was the very best perfume you see.

Rotten: But that's a bananas thing to do... *(Unsure.)* Isn't it? Is that why Simon was angry?

Jemima: He thought it was a waste. But when you *really* love someone and you're *really* sorry, the cost doesn't matter. Especially for Jesus. Nothing but the best is good enough for him. Some things may seem crazy – what did you call it – bananas? But sometimes those things are exactly what God wants. *(Pause.)* I suppose I'd better be getting back now...

Ripe: *(Dreamily.)* It is a nice smell. It's Chanel Number Five, or there again it could be Anais Anais...

Rotten: Makes you think though, dunnit? I wonder if *I've* ever been that sorry for the things I've done?

(Ripe and Rotten exit thoughtfully.)

* TALK TIME * TALK TIME * TALK TIME *

For this talk, you will need a small bottle of perfume. The Cabin Crew will need to be prepared for questions afterwards. They should have a Good News Bible *and a few copies of* The Good News *handy. It can be copied from the master on page 62. Remind team members to make a note of any children who are given a copy, so that they can be followed up.*

(Sniffs.) That perfume does smell nice, doesn't it? This perfume has a nice smell too. *(Hold up bottle.)* But unfortunately, perfume is mega expensive. It's very difficult to make and it takes a long time, so even a tiny bottle will cost loads of money. That's why it's often kept for *very* special occasions. So pouring a *whole bottle* all over someone's feet wasn't just a bit bananas – it was *really* bananas. But if you love someone very much, you don't care about the cost. You want to do everything you can. You want to give them the best. You want to make them really happy.

It's a bit like that with God too. He loves us very, very much and he wants the best for us, so he gave us something precious. It was Jesus. We've been learning about Jesus this week – Jesus, God's only son. Because he loves us, God let Jesus be punished *instead of us* for all the wrong things in our lives. How was Jesus punished? *(Ask the Passengers if they know.)* Yes, he was killed. He was put on a cross to die. That's how Jesus took the blame for us, so that we can be let off.

In fact, you could say, 'God went bananas for us!' His only son, Jesus, was really special, but he let him be killed! What a waste! That's what they said about the perfume, wasn't it? But it wasn't a waste at all. It cost God a lot. Everything, in fact, but it meant that with all the wrong things in our lives over and dealt with, we can be friends with God. Of course, that wasn't the end of the story. After three days, Jesus came back to life again and now he's alive for ever and ever.

God wants us to be his friends. Some people might say *you've* gone bananas if you become God's friend, but in fact it's the most sensible, very best thing you could do. If you want to know more, ask me or one of your Cabin Crew afterwards. They would love to have a quick chat with you just before you go home.

* TALK TIME * TALK TIME * TALK TIME *

POSTCARD HOME

Dear

Today I went to GOING BANANAS!

Banana Splits
☐ served yummy refreshments
☐ sang a song
☐ made us do the washing up.

made ☐ a brilliant costume
☐ a new friend ☐ a mess.

liked ☐ Banana Skins ☐ the Time Shed
☐ Rip yer socks off!

We learnt that a lady in the Bible went bananas and poured expensive perfume on Jesus' feet. The best thing I discovered about God was that...

....

....

Lots of love from

JEMIMA

Here are two pictures about today's story. They are both the same — or are they? Can you spot ten differences? Circle them when you find them.

All-age worship

I deally, this will be the 'Grand Finale' and will give everyone a taste of **GOING BANANAS!** You will need to invite the Passengers to join an extra flight to Banana Island and extend the invitation to their families. Perhaps you could print special invitations, and even deliver some personally – it's an ideal opportunity to visit the homes and make contact with parents. If it's held in your church building, it will be a good way of getting children who do not attend church to come along with their parents and brothers and sisters. Hopefully they will have a really positive experience of actually being in a church building!

The actual 'service' itself should be as similar to the other five days as possible. Although it will involve a lot of work, it is worth making the effort to transport as much of the set as you can. If it is re-assembled in the church, it adds to the atmosphere. The trees made on Day 4 could be fixed to chairs or the ends of pews, and some of the other things the Passengers made in their Banana Bunches could be displayed around the walls. With the Banana band playing and all the team in their t-shirts or costumes, it should be just like the real thing! Perhaps the Banana Splits team could make some special refreshments for the end of the service. Even Passport Control could operate as usual and the Passengers could sit with the Cabin Crew in their Banana Bunches.

The programme could include most of the usual elements, with a quick re-cap of the main teaching points from each day's story. A suggested outline could be as follows:

9.45
The Passengers arrive, some with their families. After being welcomed at the door by the Airport Staff, they register at Passport Control and look at the displays on the wall.

9.55
The Banana Band play some of the favourite songs from the week while people are arriving.

10.00
The Banana Band lead the **GOING BANANAS!** song.

10.05
The Captain explains about the flight procedure as usual and everyone flies to Banana Island.

10.10
The Banana Boys appear, introduce themselves and then do the **GOING BANANAS!** shout. They do a quick re-cap on the week, asking the Passengers to tell everyone about some of the things in the programme which they enjoyed. Five Passengers could bring their Postcards Home and read out one each, covering all five days. (This will need to be prepared in advance.)

10.20
Song, followed by Bananabrains with The Banana Piranha. The quiz operates in exactly the same way as on Day 3. The questions are True or False, as before, using the cards and putting bananas in the basket. The Banana Piranha appears and tries to grab bananas before he is seen. If they cover each of the stories, the questions will be a good way to re-cap on the week's teaching. (If possible, some questions should use the actual Bible passages in some way, as there is no Bible reading as such.)

10.40
The Banana Boys explain a simple routine for Banana Skins, such as standing up, turning around twice and sitting down again. Then they could find the last Message in a Bottle from Day 4, get a Passenger to fish it out of the 'sea' and read out some messages. They could finish with a time of prayer, reading out any prayer messages written by the Passengers or Cabin Crew. (If there aren't any, they could write some new messages there and then, with help from the audience, before praying them altogether.)

10.50
The Banana Boys blow the whistle for Banana Skins. When it has finished and everyone has finally sat down, they could blow it again!

10.52
The Navigator gives a brief talk at this point summing up the week's teaching, focusing on what God is like (referring to the speech bubbles which could be on display) and explaining why **GOING BANANAS!** for God is actually the most sensible thing anyone can do.

10.58
Finish with a prayer and the **GOING BANANAS!** song before Banana Splits. Make sure you have advertised any follow-up events. While everyone is having refreshments, you could chat to the families and mention whatever will be happening next.

further resources

SUGGESTED SONG LIST:

Song	Author and source	Publisher
Be bold, be strong	*Morris Chapman* *Songs of Fellowship*	Kingsway Music
Going Bananas	*Rachael Jones* **GOING BANANAS!**	Scripture Union
Great, great, brill, brill	*Doug Horley* *Jesus is the Boss*	Thankyou Music
I'm special	*Graham Kendrick* *Mission Praise 2*	Thankyou Music
I reach up high	*Judy Bailey* *Spring Harvest Kids' Praise 1995*	Daybreak Music
I will sing and celebrate	*Richard Hubbard* *A Rich Feast*	Thankyou Music
Jesus is greater	*Gill Hutchinson* *Spring Harvest Kids' Praise 1992*	Daybreak Music
Shoop, shoop	*Paul Crouch/David Mudie* *Spring Harvest Kids' Praise 1995*	Daybreak Music

SUGGESTED BOOKS OF PRAYERS:

Title	Author	Publisher
Best Loved Prayers	*Compiled by Lois Rock*	Lion Publishing
365 Children's Prayers	*Carol Watson*	Lion Publishing
101 Ideas for Creative Prayers	*Judith Merrell*	Scripture Union
My Own Book of Prayers	*Compiled by Mary Batchelor*	Lion Publishing
Talking to God	*Margaret Barfield*	Scripture Union

OTHER RESOURCE BOOKS:

Title	Author	Publisher
The Adventure Begins	*Terry Clutterham*	Scripture Union
How to Cheat at Visual Aids	*Pauline Adams and Judith Merrell*	Scripture Union
Nuts and Bolts	*Steve Hutchinson*	Scripture Union
Reaching Children	*Paul Butler*	Scripture Union

This simple gospel outline could be photocopied onto small pieces of card. The Navigator, Captain, Banana Boys and Cabin Crew could have several copies each, to use as appropriate.

THE GOOD NEWS

Find Romans 5:8,10a in your Bible.

- God created people to be perfect and obey him.
- Instead they chose to please themselves. They disobeyed God and did wrong, so their friendship with God was spoilt because he is holy.
- Ever since then the wrong things that people think, say and do have kept them from being friends with God.
- Because Jesus took the punishment we deserved when he died on the cross, we can become God's friends. He will forgive us for all the wrong things we think, say and do if we ask him to.

- Then we receive the Holy Spirit, the special 'helper' from God who helps us to be holy and to live to please him.
(Romans 5:8,10a)

If you want to become one of God's friends, you could pray this simple prayer:

- Thank you, God, that you love me and will forgive me.
- Sorry for the wrong things I think, say and do.
- Please, Lord Jesus, come into my life and be my special friend.

SPEECH BUBBLE MASTER

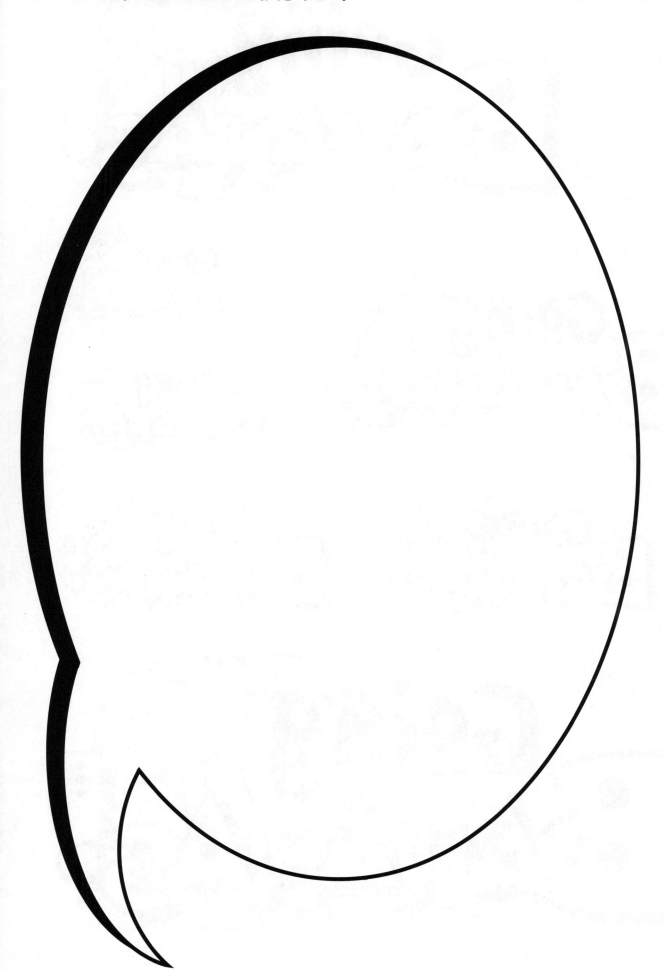

LOGOS